HERBS

HERBS

EXCITING RECIPES FOR COOKING WITH HERBS

LINDA TUBBY PHOTOGRAPHY BY PETER CASSIDY

RYLAND
PETERS
& SMALL

LONDON NEW YORK

First published in the United States in 2004
by Ryland Peters & Small, Inc.
519 Broadway, 5th Floor
New York, NY 10012
www.rylandpeters.com

10 9 8 7 6 5 4 3 2 1

Library of Congress Cataloging-in-Publication Data

Tubby, Linda.
  Herbs : exciting recipes for cooking with herbs /
Linda Tubby ;
photography by Peter Cassidy.
    p. cm.
Includes index.
  ISBN 1-84172-568-4
  1. Cookery (Herbs) 2. Herbs. I. Title.
TX819.H4T82 2004
641.6'57--dc22
                            2003021083

Printed and bound in China

Dedication

For my sons Dan and Ben, with love.

Acknowledgments

My thanks go first to photographer Peter Cassidy,
whose lovely and sensitive work has made this book
so special. To Kate, his assistant, without whom we
would all be lost—bless you. Special thanks to Elsa
for being a most encouraging and supportive editor,
and so knowledgeable about all sorts of odd things.
To Steve Painter, for all his creative thoughts,
enthusiasm, and superb book designing (he also
knows a thing or two about gardening, which was
handy). To Róisín Nield, for beautiful prop styling and
always knowing just
what to bring.

Dan at Mortimer and Bennet for his food advice. Phil,
Gary, and Eddie at Covent Garden Fisheries for
always ensuring I had pretty happy fish. Phalida Chard
for all things Thai. Paul Gayler for being such a good
influence, to many more people who gave advice, and
to Lesley Faddy for rocket fuel and more.

My family, for putting up with herb pots and for doing
without regular meals. My Mam, my friends, and
supporters, who are forever there and great. Jerry, for
techy support. Finally, thanks to those wonderful herbs
for always being right outside my door. Everyone at
Ryland Peters & Small, who have been so helpful,
especially Sharon Ashman for her help with editing,
and Gabriella le Grazie for her basil enthusiasm.

Senior Designer Steve Painter
Commissioning Editor Elsa Petersen-Schepelern
Production Patricia Harrington
Art Director Gabriella Le Grazie
Publishing Director Alison Starling

Food Stylist Linda Tubby
Stylist Róisín Nield
Indexer Diana LeCore

Notes

• All spoon measurements are level unless
otherwise stated.

• Ingredients in this book are available from larger
supermarkets, specialty produce markets, garden
centers, and nurseries. See page 142 for mail order
sources.

• Fresh herbs are preferred for the recipes in this
book, and most are available year round. If using
dried herbs for any reason, use about one-third of
the measure mentioned. Some herbs, such as
thyme, tarragon, oregano, and bay leaves have
specific uses in their dried forms, so buy them from
a source with a fast turnover. Like spices, they lose
pungency with age, so buy little and often.

• Ovens should be preheated to the specified
temperature. Recipes in this book were tested using
a conventional oven. If using a convexion oven,
cooking times should be changed according to the
manufacturer's instructions.

• For all recipes requiring dough or batter, liquid
measurements are given as a guide. Always add
liquid gradually to achieve the desired consistency,
rather than adding it all at once. Use your eyes and
your sense of touch to achieve the best results. If
you don't use the type of flour specified in a recipe,
the result may be affected.

CONTENTS

INTRODUCTION

Fresh herbs have such a natural appeal in the kitchen, adding a vast range of exciting flavor dimensions to the dishes we cook. With so many exotic fresh herbs now available from all over the world, and all the hundreds of different varieties we can grow at home, cooking with herbs has never been so inspiring. They thrill with their visual beauty and a variety of sensational aromas—from rounded cushions of wild oregano on hot Greek hillsides to the creamy-white, frothy feminine flower heads of sweet cicely growing by streams and along country roadsides in springtime. Once seen, who can forget fields of French lavender growing in swathes across the landscape, or Italian basil with shiny, brilliant-green leaves growing in abundance, just waiting to enliven a dish of ripe tomatoes? I loved browsing through the markets of Southeast Asia, which groan with huge bunches of flowering chives, lemongrass, and Thai basil, so firm and fresh, just begging to give their heady aroma to flavor a tangy stir-fry or curry.

Fresh herbs are preferred for the recipes in this book, and most are available year round. However, this wasn't always so, and various forms of drying have been evolved, all of which try to preserve the flavor, aroma, and (formerly) the medicinal qualities of the herbs in question. Some, especially woody herbs, respond well to drying. Other, softer ones, such as basil, don't. A modern invention, freeze-drying, has improved their prospects somewhat, but I think that, if possible, use herbs fresh. This is not to ignore the fact that some, such as thyme, tarragon, oregano, and bay leaves, do have specific uses in their dried forms, so if you plan to cook recipes using this form of herb, buy from a source with a fast turnover. Like spices, dried herbs lose pungency with age, so buy little and often.

Herbs have been around as a natural resource for many thousands of years. Many of them started out life in the sunny climate of the Mediterranean and were carried to other parts of the world by invaders and explorers, who spread the seeds of many of the familiar herbs we use today.

All these wonderful fresh herbs we now have at our green fingertips bring a special flavor to our cooking endeavors as well as an extra hidden dimension— they help our bodies deal with the food we eat and bring added vitamins and minerals to our diet. In days gone by, people gradually acquired an understanding of herbs both for their culinary and medicinal uses—a wisdom passed on from generation to generation. Sage was known to aid digestion so it was added to rich foods; thyme, because of its powerful antiseptic qualities, was used to marinate meat to stop it spoiling long before refrigeration; and dill was used to ease the pain of teething infants and to aid digestion.

The Romans especially used herbs not only in their food but also to nurture mind, body, and spirit. Their huge armies made great use of them, for at that time, herbs were the only medicines available. It's exciting to know that herbs are as adaptable as ever they were, playing their dual role for us today in both food and medicine.

KNOW YOUR HERBS

bay leaves

hyssop

lavender

rosemary

savory

thyme

STRONG WOODY HERBS

Bay leaves come from the same family as avocado and cinnamon. The bay tree was originally a wild plant of the Mediterranean, where it thrives more pungently and powerfully than anywhere else. Greek and Roman heroes were crowned with wreaths of bay leaves as a symbol of excellence.

When you crush the leaves, the aromas range from grassy and floral to bitter—as a flavoring herb, they stand up to long cooking, which brings out their sweet mellowness.

Infuse a leaf or two in milk and cream for savory or sweet dishes, or use a sprig in a bowl of red wine marinade with garlic and onions. When cooking cabbage, cauliflower, or other strong-smelling vegetables, add a bay leaf to diminish the odor.

Rosemary has been a culinary and medicinal herb since ancient Greek and Roman times. The Romans thought so highly of it they dedicated it to Venus, the Goddess of Love. It is also thought to improve the memory—as Ophelia said so sadly in Shakespeare's *Hamlet*, "rosemary is for remembrance."

Apart from the classic partnerships with roast lamb and monkfish, the leaves are also capable of delivering some delicious flavors to desserts. Put the flowers or leaves in a pot of sugar for two weeks, and use to make meringues or syrups, or warm the leaves and flowers with honey to pour over figs, melon, or orange salad.

Sage—from the Latin word *salvere*, meaning "to save"—was and still is a highly valued medicinal herb, as well as a prime candidate for the award for one of the best culinary herbs.

It is known as the "herb of the heart" and—even more astonishing—chewing the leaves is said to make teeth white and shiny.

Sage is a popular herb in many regions of Italy. Its pungent robustness adds a new dimension to buttery dishes and many others, including my own favorite—rare char-grilled calves' liver with sage leaves fried in melted butter with a little dusting of hot paprika on the plate. In Tuscany, butter is infused with sage to serve with ravioli and gnocchi.

In Germany, it is cooked with eel, helping the digestive system cope with the richness of the dish. It makes a delicious flavoring for apple jelly to serve with pork, rich potato dishes with cream are transformed, while the flowers can be used to flavor bread dough, or to decorate the top of the loaf.

Sage, like many woody herbs, can stand up to long, slow cooking without losing its strength. In spring, sage has a gentle, mild aroma, but by the summer, when the flowers are just in bud, its volatile oils have matured in the heat of the sun. This is the combination that can create the "medicine cabinet" effect that is too overpowering for food, unless used with a delicate hand.

To care for sage, put bunches of leaves in a pitcher of shallow water with just the very

ends of the stalks in the water, put a plastic bag over the top and, when the leaves have perked up, take the bag off and leave the pitcher of herbs on the kitchen table as an edible decoration. I like to keep them this way rather than in the refrigerator, where the leaves turn limp and sad.

Purple sage can be used as common sage, but it is not as pungent, so it is good sautéed, or dipped in batter and deep-fried.

Pineapple sage has red-edged, pointed, oval leaves with red stems and scarlet flowers in winter. Early in the season the leaves have a strong pineapple flavor when crushed. This flavor diminishes after flowering. Use the leaves instead of tansy in the Panna Cotta recipe on page 123. There are many scented sages you can plant in your garden, and they are worth some experimentation as culinary ammunition.

Savory or *sarriete*—its charming French name—was introduced into northern Europe by the Romans, who used this highly aromatic herb as a peppery, spicy flavoring. It was commonly used to ease digestion after the enjoyment of certain challenging foods and, as if that weren't enough, it was also considered an aphrodisiac.

Summer savory is an annual and is known as the bean herb because it eases flatulence. The flavor of the tender leaves is similar to thyme. I like to use the leaves and flowers—white or pale pink—with beans, lentils, grilled fish, and vegetables.

Winter savory is evergreen, with lilac or white flowers, and is a little stronger and a bit more resinous than summer savory, with a flavor similar to thyme. It suits bean dishes as well as grilled meat and fish. A commercially grown savory is now available in supermarkets but it hasn't the same strength as homegrown.

Thyme from the Greek *thymos*—"to perfume"—has so many varieties, full of character and all with their own subtle aroma and flavor.

The ancient Egyptians and Greeks knew the powerful antiseptic and preservative qualities of thyme, and its ability to stimulate the brain and improve the memory. Roman cooks used it to preserve their meat: those strong antiseptic qualities delayed it spoiling.

In the 17th century, cooking with thyme was believed to make fairies visible—I like that.

Lemon thyme tastes strongly of citrus and is delicious broiled with peaches and figs or stuffed inside a fish. Add a few sprigs to a marinade for lamb, along with oil and black pepper—let chill in the refrigerator for 24 hours, adding salt for the last 30 minutes as you let the lamb return to room temperature before cooking.

Hyssop, a common Mediterranean shrub, was a sacred herb in ancient Greece. It is a good foil for rich pork dishes and oily fish, because it aids digestion. The leaves have a minty, anise-like flavor with a little sage note, while the white, pink, or purple flowers have a minty taste. The leaves are still quite potent in winter and add a warm spiciness to poached fruits.

When chopped and used as a rub, its strength is the perfect partner for game dishes. But take care—like all the woody herbs, its strength varies depending on the season, and a heavy hand can ruin a dish.

Lavender was highly prized by the Greeks and Romans, who liked the scent and healing qualities in their bath water—its name is derived from the Latin *lavare*, meaning "to wash." Though lavender has always been considered terribly English, my memories of France are of lavender, with drifts of it coloring the view to infinity.

The culinary talents of lavender have been known for centuries and it's becoming a top herb again. Use the flowers to flavor sugar and to make cookies, syrups, ice creams, and in a more savory context for stuffing and sauces. Well-known British chef Paul Gayler, of London's Lanesborough hotel, grinds down the buds and calls it "pollen," which he mixes with butter and puts under the skin of a chicken to roast—quite delicious. I grind the flowers with salt and use as a rub for meat. Use the leaves to flavor game, and roast with a leg of lamb as you would rosemary. It's very potent, so use it sparingly.

I have a soft spot for the fresh blossoms, which I snatch from under the bees' noses and scatter over summer strawberries along with a dusting of scented sugar (the berries can take the overkill) and a dollop of whipped cream.

Lavender was used in love spells to attract men. So if you feel the need, get out your cooking pots and start weaving the magic.

SOFT LEAFY HERBS

Basil takes its name from the Greek *basileus*, meaning "king." It is native to India, where it is sacred and known as *tulsi*. It was first brought to Egypt around 3,000 years ago, then on to Rome, and so to all parts of southern Europe. These days it grows wherever the climate suits.

Many cooks have a rule that basil must only be torn, not cut. Metal reacts with the plant juices, turning the cut edges black and bitter. If the leaf is torn, the tear takes the natural line of the cell structure.

Greek or **bush basil** is very bushy, with tiny pointed leaves and white flowers. It is grown throughout Greece in gardens or pots near doorways as a sign of welcome, and in churches it can be found just below the altar in its spiritual role as holy basil.

The common basil we know as **sweet** or **Italian basil** is not shy about throwing its peppery, minty, clove-like scent around when warmed by the sun, but when cold in the confines of the pantry it can smell of cats.

Lettuce basil is a large-leaved variety. Use whole leaves in wrappings or as stuffings, or tear them into salads.

Purple basil or **opal basil** has pinkish-purple, and in some cases almost black, leaves. If it flops, plunge into hand-hot water for 15 minutes—not only does this bring it back to life, it intensifies its color quite dramatically.

Basil is said to create understanding between people. It also has a raunchy reputation in Spain where ladies of ill repute use it to entice clients. Asia has its own family of basils, and these are listed on page 16.

Borage was taken all over Europe by the Roman legions. Roman soldiers believed it gave them great courage—something obviously worked, as they rampaged their way across the known world for over 500 years.

Young, fresh borage has strong cucumber-flavored leaves—delicious dipped in light batter and deep-fried. Float the star-like purple flowers in drinks or freeze them in ice cubes to chill summer drinks—a classic with the English favorite, Pimm's.

Chervil was introduced as a flavoring herb to western Europe by the invading Roman legions. They carried it from the Caucasus and the Middle East to western Europe where it settled into common use, especially in France and Belgium. It is part of the herb quartet that flavors the classic French dish *omelette au fines herbes*—to which its contribution is important, because a little chervil accentuates the flavor of the other three herbs. It makes a delicate soup, and when added to young carrots, it reaches dizzy heights.

Always add chervil to a hot dish at the very last moment because its flavor is destroyed by prolonged cooking. Use the tangles of lacy leaves in salads to maximize invaluable nutritional benefits.

Chervil has a sweet, mildly anise flavor, with a twang of fruity wine. Though it looks delicate, it's a brave little herb, and when grown in the garden, is a good deal hardier than any commercially grown specimen. It was available in supermarkets for a while, but the poor little thing wasn't quite strong enough for the tough packaged life. You can find it at good produce markets, where they know how to deal with its delicate demeanor.

basil

chervil

cilantro

dill

fennel

lovage

Cilantro is the herb mentioned in the Bible and in Sanskrit texts, and was also found in Egyptian tombs in seed form (coriander). Its popularity has stood the test of time, considering it has also had the worst press in the world. We love it and hate it with equal passion. I'm firmly in the former camp, but feel I always have to ask if everyone likes it before mixing handfuls into a dish. Although cilantro must not be cooked to death, it really needs that brief assignation with the warmth of the food to bring out its fullness. On the other hand, its idiosyncratic flavor in fresh salsa is not to be missed.

Cilantro was brought to Europe by late bronze-age nomads to flavor their barley gruel, while the Spaniards carried it to Mexico and Peru, where it became an indispensable partner to their much loved chile. In Britain, it was commercially grown in the 19th century for the seed, which was used as a supporting flavor for gin.

Dill started out in the Middle East in biblical times. It migrated with travelers into Europe, North and South America, further east into Asia, as well as north to Scandinavia.

Its name comes appropriately from the old Norse word *dylla* meaning "to lull." The leaves have a sweet, almost alcoholic flavor, with vague hints of anise that aren't as strong as fennel, but similar to caraway in taste.

It is used in Scandinavia with salmon, carrots, and beets or tossed into new potatoes with butter. Polish cooks use it with sour cream, hard-cooked eggs, and pickles. The Greeks like to partner it with fava beans, and in Iran it's

eaten raw, along with other herbs on the table, throughout the meal. Dill is used as a vegetable in Southeast Asia, where it's always cooked, and goes by the name *paksi* or *pak chi lao*.

Graceful **fennel**, with its feathery foliage under an umbrella of yellow flowers, was used by the Greeks to suppress the appetite.

Fennel will keep in a plastic bag in the refrigerator for four days providing it's not wet, when it becomes slimy very quickly.

Fennel is the perfect herb stuffed inside or sprinkled on top of oily fish, and the clean fresh flavor is delicious tossed through a bowl of grilled vegetables.

Lovage, sometimes known as sea parsley (it grows wild on sea cliffs and coastlines), has a strong celery scent, and is known for its "meaty" protein flavor. When young, the leaves taste salty and lemony, and are good in salads or with vegetable and bean casseroles. When the plant grows tall and the leaves become slightly bitter, use them just for stews.

It is good with potato soup and I love it cooked in the oven with lentils and onions.

Like many herbs, lovage was grown in the earliest monastic physic gardens for medicinal purposes. It was thought to be good for digestive problems and to relieve stomach cramps. At one time it was thought to be an aphrodisiac—hence the name.

Mint was introduced to Europe by the Romans and has remained the most popular herb in the world. Peppermint tea, of course, is the drink of

choice throughout the Middle East since it is as stimulating as coffee. It was said to restore and revive the spirit and excite the appetite.

Infuse the leaves in boiling water for five minutes to overcome nausea. Add to green tea as in Morocco, or use in iced mint tea, which you make by adding a handful of bruised mint leaves to a pot of Chinese green tea, along with the juice of a lime and some honey. Chill well, adding ice cubes, if you like. Another great summer drink is mint julep—mash mint leaves with sugar and mix with crushed ice and bourbon.

Spearmint or garden mint is used in classic mint sauce with roast lamb. The perfect mint sauce is made by pouring boiling water over a handful of chopped mint with sugar. Let cool, then add cider vinegar to taste and serve with a silver or non-reactive spoon. Mint is also a favorite in kabobs, the comfort food of the Middle East, the raita of India, and the *sauce paloise* of France.

Apple mint has a soft gray-green fleshy leaf with a wonderful apple mint aroma and flavor. Use whole sprigs when cooking peas, potatoes, and beans.

Sweet marjoram, now found all over the Mediterranean and western Asia, was introduced to Europe in the Middle Ages from North Africa. Use in dishes that don't need lengthy cooking, such as soufflés and light food. The leaves become floppy quickly, so add to salads at the last minute. Marjoram's generic name is "oregano," while confusingly, oregano's other name is "wild marjoram." Sweet marjoram looks delicate with light-green, soft leaves and a

marjoram

oregano

mint

flat-leaf parsley

sweet cicely

tarragon

beige–pink stalk. The leaves are sweetly scented, with white or pinky purple flowers. It has a more fleshy and tender look to it than the stronger looking relative, pot marjoram, also known as French marjoram.

The antiseptic qualities for which this genus was famous meant that it was used as a strewing herb–scattered around kitchens to keep them sweet-smelling. As a result, it was a prominent crop in the kitchen gardens from Renaissance times.

I have grown pot marjoram for many years and it looks very similar to oregano, except the leaves are a lighter green and the flowers tend to be paler. Having a slightly tougher leaf than sweet marjoram, it can be used more robustly in tomato sauces and dishes that are cooked a little longer. I use it in a meatball mix together with mint and pine nuts.

Golden marjoram has a very soft, pale, green-gold leaf with white flowers. It grows so well for me in big fat pillows and is so lush that it's difficult for me to cut into it. But this I must do, since the flavor is excellent and stands up well to cooking when added ten minutes before the end of the cooking time.

Oregano, or wild marjoram, as it is sometimes known, is a woody perennial, and the hotter the sun, the stronger the flavor. This genus belongs to the mint family. Italians use the flower heads just before they bloom, as well as the leaves, to flavor dishes.

The many wild species of oregano are known collectively as "rigani," which grow pungently in the wild on hillsides and mountains throughout Greece. It's the wild species (not grown commercially), which is harvested when in bud and dried for maximum aroma. We love to bring it back from vacations in Greece, by the suitcase-full.

In Latin America and the Mediterranean, oregano is used as we use parsley. It is an essential ingredient in Italian cooking and a favorite herb in Greek cuisine—where would they be without it for tomato sauces and salads?

Parsley was a native of the eastern Mediterranean and was brought to Western Europe in the 16th century where it began to grow so naturally and happily in rough places that it became known as "rock celery." The Greeks considered parsley to have too many associations with the devil, so preferred to keep its use to the medicine cabinet. The Romans, however, were happy to cook with it—how clued up they were—and it is now considered the most indispensable culinary herb.

Flat-leaf parsley (or French, Italian, or Continental parsley, as it's often called) is essential to many traditional flavoring mixtures. My favorite is Italian gremolata—a mix of parsley, chopped garlic, and lemon zest, which is sprinkled over finished dishes. The French version is *persillade*, traditionally without lemon.

One of my favorite uses of parsley is in *beurre de gascogne*—lots of blanched garlic and freshly chopped parsley mixed with duck or goose fat, and mixed into a simple cassoulet at the last moment. I make *salmoriglio*—a mixture of salt, garlic, lemon juice, olive oil, and parsley, which is fabulous for sardines and with fresh anchovies. Parsley (and mint) is also the essential herb in tabbouleh, where classically the herbs are the dish, and the grains of bulghur are there simply to stop the juices from the other ingredients falling to the bottom of the bowl.

Curly leaf parsley isn't the most fashionable herb these days, and many discount it, but the flavor, when well grown, is iron-laden and sweet. I love it deep-fried to a crispness, so it crumbles in the mouth like Cantonese crispy seaweed. It also holds up well to cooking in stuffing, but must be finely chopped, or the texture can be prickly. If you grow it at home, make sure the leaves are picked when tender. Like other parsley varieties, it contains masses of chlorophyll, the bright-green leaf juice which is packed with goodness.

Sweet cicely, sometimes known as licorice root, is a native of northern Europe. This is an herb you must grow yourself, because, as yet, no one sells it by the bunch. This is a shame— its qualities demand that it should be in more prominent use. Its firm, chervil-like leaves and froth of white flowers have a sweet anise and licorice flavor, so it tastes very good in all things sweet. It loves the companionship of sharp fruits in dishes like crumbles, reducing the acidity, so you need less sugar.

Add the leaves to vegetable soups right at the end of cooking to sweeten and bring out their flavor. I like the leaves in green salads and with broiled goat cheese. The leaves and flowers also make fantastic tempura with extra leaves infused in a syrup, then strained to use as a dip.

Tansy is a native of Europe and the Greeks and Romans considered it a symbol of immortality. To my mind, it's another herb like cilantro, either it's loved or loathed. It is very deep in flavor—quite unforgettable. Tansy was the name of the herb as well as the name of the pudding it flavored—eaten at Easter time, often in the form of bread-like cakes. At other times it appeared in rich mousse-like creamy puddings. Rubbed on lamb, it gives a similar flavor to rosemary. In the 17th century, it was stir-fried with oranges and sugar.

Tansy has strong antiseptic qualities and before there was such a thing as refrigeration, it was used to wrap meat to repel flies. I use only the very young leaves for flavoring the dessert on page 123. Like many bitter herbs, it has a reputation for being a digestive stimulant—sensitive souls may prefer to substitute bay or thyme instead.

Tarragon is the aristocrat of the herb garden. The aromatic, shiny, smooth, light-green leaves are the only soft leaf herb that can withstand long cooking. In fact, I think cooking it mellows and warms the flavor, losing the harsher side of its character. This herb makes famous pairings with chicken or rich cream sauces. The pungent, bossy, anise flavor turns saintly and mellow after 30 minutes in the oven with chicken pieces, white wine, and heavy cream. Remove the branch of tarragon towards the end of cooking and add a second hit of it about five minutes before the end of the cooking time.

The flavor of tarragon is at its most pungent in high summer. It can have a numbing effect on the tongue when chewed raw, and is quite alcoholic in flavor—like pastis, but without the water to temper its strength.

Many gardeners have been disappointed when they discover they have the tasteless Russian variety, rather than the glorious French. Take care when you buy small plants—scratch and sniff the leaves to make sure.

Tarragon is one of those herbs that survives the drying process. French roast chicken with dried tarragon is delicious—the version in which many people first taste this wonderful herb.

THE ONION FAMILY

Garlic is the ultimate herb grown for flavoring and as a vegetable in its own right. The active substance in garlic is aiilicun, which comes to the fore when the cloves are chopped or crushed, this is the medicinally active part and creates the garlic odor. Garlic is at its most beneficial to health when eaten raw, but still retains many benefits when cooked. Russians eat it to keep old age at bay.

If you grow your own, divide the cloves from the bulb and plant them in fall for the next year. They produce a delicious crop, and also keep insects away from other plants. Young green garlic is useful in many dishes for its mild flavor and also makes a delicious soup. Extreme temperature change can cause garlic to take on a hotter taste. The variety grown in Thailand has a less pungent flavor than its Western relative. Leave some plants to flower—they are beautiful with large pompoms, like big chive flowers.

Chives were brought back to Europe from the East by Marco Polo in the 13th century and have since become indispensable in the kitchen, in the same way as garlic and onions. Some people say they shouldn't be cooked, but I find they are a perfect flavoring for soufflés and savory tarts with fillings based on eggs, cream, or cheese. Where would we be without chives sprinkled over new potatoes or chopped up over hot baked potato with sour cream?

If you're a gardener, there are many varieties available, some with white flowers, but the common chive with its lilac-pink pompom flower heads is hard to beat. I use these flowers all through the spring, to scatter over salads and grilled dishes, or any dish where a hint of onion flavor works.

After cutting the leaves from the plant, wrap them in damp paper towels, then put them in a plastic bag and store in the vegetable drawer of the refrigerator.

Chinese chives, also known as garlic chives, have been cultivated for centuries in China, Japan, and Vietnam. One variety has flat leaves and is sold either with just leaves, or with the large buds or flowers. They give a mild garlic flavor and can be used like common chives or in stir-fries and rice dishes. These can be bought from Asian stores, bound in long bundles.

Also in Chinese markets, you will find a variety that is blanched under cloches to whiten them, and these are considered a delicacy.

Flowering chives or **kuchai** are grown specifically for their flowering stems, in bud or flower form. The stems and flowers are chopped into stir-fry dishes. These have an ultra-powerful, pungently garlic smell, a bit like wild garlic, but cooking tempers the smell and flavor.

In Europe, wild garlic or ramsons with its spear-like leaves is found growing wild in muddy, shady places. In North America, **ramps** or **wild leeks** are similar. Take care when gathering them, and wash thoroughly before use. They are also sometimes cultivated and, in season, are sometimes sold in gourmet stores. Both flowers and leaves are edible, but the leaves are best eaten before the plant flowers.

Use the leaves as a wrapping for steamed fish. The stunning starry flowers have a pungent flavor and are good used in a salad of bitter leaves tossed with goat cheese and nuts.

CITRUS FLAVORED HERBS

Lemon verbena, a native of Chile and Argentina, was brought to Europe in the 18th century by the Spaniards. It has strong, lance-shaped leaves with an intensely fresh lemon aroma, which is at its best when the flowers are on the verge of blooming. However, even in winter, the few remaining dried-out leaves left on a plant still retain a strong fragrance when crushed.

Use lemon verbena in fish dishes and with duck. I infuse the leaves in cream to make panna cotta (page 123) and use it to poach peaches in summer, and infuse in sugar and chilled wine to make a syllabub for the topping. A few of the delicate pink flowers sprinkled over the top reinforces the flavor.

To help insomnia, make a tisane (herb tea) from crushed fresh leaves, and sip the strained liquid last thing at night.

Lemon balm is also known as balm, lime balm, bee balm, or melissa (the Greek word for honey bee). The plants were used by bee keepers in the 17th and 18th centuries to keep their bees well behaved and close to the hives.

The serrated, slightly hairy leaves look very much like small nettle leaves, and in summer the plant is covered with tiny white flowers. The aroma can be quite overpowering in old, tough plants, especially those grown in pots.

Lemon balm is wonderful for flavoring vinegar, gelatins, vegetables, fresh fruits, and cold drinks.

In the 13th century, lemon balm was mixed with honey and used to make a tisane. It was said to chase away dark thoughts, strengthen a stressed nervous system, and, above all, to keep you young. Today, herbalists still use it to calm and soothe.

Vietnamese balm, is grown and used in the US. Although not from the same family as lemon balm, it has similar attributes and could be used as a substitute.

Remember also **lemon geranium** (below), **kaffir lime leaves**, and **lemongrass** (page 16). Other herbs have varieties with citrus flavors, such as **lemon thyme** (page 10).

FLOWER AND FRUIT SCENTED HERBS

Scented geranium leaves have an intense scent associated with the variety. **Rose** smells of roses, **lemon** of lemon, and there are **apple, mint,** or **nutmeg** scented geraniums. The flowers, unlike other herbs, have no scent at all but are edible and can be used to decorate desserts or salads. Use the fresh leaves to scent sugar stored in a jar—the results can be used for puddings, syrups, meringues, ice creams, and gelatins. The leaves are pretty, pressed into the top of a cake and covered with a dusting of sugar before baking.

The botanical name of the **pot marigold** is Calendula, from the Latin *calendae*, meaning "little clock," so called because it flowers all year round in its natural habitat in the Mediterranean. It opens at sunrise and closes at sunset. This is one of my favorite herbs and my best medicinal support for cuts—calendula tincture travels with me whenever my cook's knives come too. It also has an almost magical ability to keep blackfly from my garden. I love its simple, bright, cheery flowers in orange and yellow—so good to look at in the garden, and for flavor and color in food. Fresh and dried petals have been added to the cooking pot since the Middle Ages, hence the name

"pot marigold." The flowers have a warm, peppery, salty taste and work wonders with feta cheese and pine nuts. Teamed with ricotta in a stuffing for zucchini flowers, they are sublime, and good in herb omelets, too. The color produced from the petals is the poor man's saffron, giving a wonderful orange tone with a subtle flavor, though not quite as spicily pungent as saffron.

Nasturtium is a relative of watercress and is also known as Indian cress. It is a native of South America, introduced into Spain from Peru in the 16th century and reaching other European countries 100 years later. Flowers and leaves have an intense, pungent, mustardy, peppery flavor. The flamboyant yellow, orange, and red of the flowers make them the ideal spicy snap for many recipes, especially salads—and they look beautiful, too.

Viola, also known as wild pansy, heartsease, or Johnny jump-up, is a native of Europe. The common name "pansy" is from the French word *pensée,* meaning a thought or remembrance of love. Although you shouldn't eat too many at once, they are good in salads, in stuffing, or candied and used to decorate desserts.

An infusion made from viola flowers was said to mend a broken heart.

Sweet violets are the purple violets classically used to flavor violet cream chocolates.

shiso leaf

epazote

curry leaf

kaffir lime leaf

lemongrass

vietnamese coriander (laksa leaf)

EXOTIC NEW ARRIVALS

More and more unusual herbs appear in our restaurants and cookbooks as chefs and food writers travel the world, and immigrants open eateries in their new countries. Whenever you see these ingredients for sale, ask the shopkeeper how they are used and how to cook with them. They will always be helpful, and all good cooks are imbued with the spirit of adventure.

Lemongrass can be grown in a greenhouse, or outdoors if you live in a mild climate. It's also widely available in Asian markets. Use the bottom 2 inches or so of the bulb, and peel off the outer couple of leaves. Either bruise the whole grass and remove it before serving, or cut it very finely, then mash even more finely with a mortar and pestle. Lemongrass stalks can also be used as kabob sticks. Freeze what you don't use—it can be used straight from frozen.

Kaffir lime leaves are the beautiful dark, glossy green leaves found in Thai curry spice packs and sold in bags in Asian markets. Again, freeze what you don't use immediately, and use straight from frozen. The leaves grow in pairs— bruise and use whole, removing before serving, or slice very finely and grind with a mortar and pestle. The word *kaffir* is old Hindi meaning "foreign." They are also known as *makrut*.

Vietnamese cilantro, often known as *rau rau* and laksa leaf, is fast becoming "the" Asian

herb. The plants can be bought from nurseries and the cut stems are available from Asian stores. Its refreshing flavor has a hot citrusy note and the cilantro-style pungency stands up well to cooking. It can be added halfway through cooking or wilted in just before serving. You can also scatter it over the dish, to serve.

The long pointed leaf has an eggplant-colored horseshoe shape in the center, making it a very attractive addition to the ubiquitous Vietnamese table salads, which are served alongside every Vietnamese meal. The leaves are also delicious deep-fried.

Its native habitat is on the banks of streams so prefers its roots to be kept moist. Its stems are succulent—a sign of a water-loving plant.

The two most commonly used **Thai sweet basils** available from Thai and other Asian stores. One has a smooth pale purple stalk with deep green, very sprightly, shiny leaves, squat purple flowers, and a strong anise and licorice aroma and flavor. The other has a brighter green leaf with a tangy, slightly lemony flavor and usually white or pale pink flowers. I have it on good authority that this one is used with fish. The edges of the leaves are smooth on both sweet basils.

Tulsi or holy basil is the sacred herb of Hindu India and believed to be Krishna's favorite plant above any garden flower. It is used as a

religious offering rather than in cooking, although it is used to make a delicious tisane.

There are two types of **Thai holy basil** available in Thai and Asian stores. The most common is the one with pale green, slightly floppy leaves, best wilted into dishes at the last moment when its subtler flavor can come to the fore. When the leaves are squeezed the aroma is very similar to that of engine oil. The other holy basil has darker leaves, pinky-purple on the top of the leaf, with deep-pink flowers. The flavor is minty and camphoric and deliciously fragrant when heated. Both these holy basils have a slightly serrated leaf.

Thai mint (*bai sarae nae*) is a very fragrant small leafed variety. It has a hottish taste with a round hairless leaf and, when mature, has a dark red stem. It is often available in Thai stores, but it is easy to propagate. Just put a stem into a glass of water until little roots show, then plant it in a pot. This is best done in spring from a bunch bought in a store with a high turnover. This variety of mint is used quite extensively throughout Southeast Asia. I find it perfect in Thai food as its spiciness gives a wonderful dimension to salads.

Vietnamese mint is used as part of the herb collection, "table salad," which is served with almost every Vietnamese meal, together with cilantro and local herbs.

Curry leaf is a musky, spicy aromatic leaf and not, as its name implies, anything like curry powder, although it is used as a component of Sri Lankan curry powder. These leaves are from a deciduous tree that grows wild in parts of India, Thailand, and Sri Lanka.

It's cultivated in southern India where it is often known as *kari patta* and used as part of a *tarka*, which is a fried mixture that also includes cumin seed, dried chiles, and asafoetida, added to a dish at the end of cooking. Curry leaves are most often used to flavor dishes rather than being eaten, although I chop them into the potato mixture for the Singaras recipe on page 134. I also deep-fry them to sprinkle on top.

Curry leaves are available in all Indian and Asian stores in sealed packs. The thin stalks have about 14 small, bright, shiny, green leaves that will keep in the refrigerator quite well for weeks. They freeze well, too.

Epazote is native to the Americas, where it grows so enthusiastically it is viewed almost as a weed. It has a pungent flavor and is often used with beans, due to its reputation as a carminative—the ability to reduce the flatulent effect of beans. Its other name, wormseed, indicates its other medicinal use.

Epazote is the important flavor in *papadzutes*, fresh corn tortillas rolled with a filling of hard-cooked eggs and swathed in the pumpkin seed sauce, mole verde—deliciously flavored with epazote. I love the odorous, pungent, hemp-like smell it gives when the leaves are squeezed, and find it quite addictive. You can also use it raw in salsas, but because of its pungency, I prefer to add it to stews and dried legumes 15 minutes before the end of cooking. It is also available as a seed, so you can grow it yourself.

Japanese shiso or **perilla** is related to the basil and mint family. It's as common in Japan as mint is in the West. There are many varieties, some nettle-like and some quite frilly. It has a mild, sweet, cumin-like aroma, and the first taste you get is similar to cumin. The afterburn is a minty spicy flavor. I'm passionate about it and want it as much as cilantro, now that I have a taste for it.

Its main use in Japan is to eat it with sashimi apparently to protect against any parasites that may be in the raw fish. Green shiso is also used in the making of sushi maki. The cultivated red shiso is used to color the famous umeboshi sour plums and is used to garnish beefsteaks, this is perhaps why it is often called the beefsteak plant. Although this could be due to its deep red color. The seeds are also sprouted in pots, creating red and green cress-like sprouts, which are great for salads. The leaves and flowering tips make wonderful herb tempura, and are also a good flavoring sliced into salads and rice. Shiso is used in Korean and Vietnamese cuisines, too.

Pandan or screwpine leaves are used to flavor and wrap food in much of Southeast Asia. The long, fresh, green leaves are around in most Asian stores and they keep for weeks if they are wrapped in a bag and stored in the vegetable drawer of the refrigerator. Bruise the leaves before using as a flavoring. It's quite floral and sweet, ideal for adding to sweet rice dishes, crêpes, and curries. I like to use the leaves to wrap fish to steam, or threaded on bamboo sticks with chicken for satays. Extract the juice from the leaves and use it as a bright green food coloring.

NOT QUITE AN HERB—ALMOST A VEGETABLE

Fenugreek leaves, also known as methi, are native to Asia and southeastern Europe. Buy fresh fenugreek in the vegetable section of Indian and Middle Eastern stores.

The bushy, silvery, olive-green leaves have a nutty, pungent, sweet curry aroma. The plant has tightly budded, pale ivory flowers and it grows a little like its relative, clover. In Iran, where it's a popular ingredient, it goes by the name of *shambaleeleh* or *shambalides*, meaning "clover-like vegetable." In Lebanese stores, it is known as *halbeh*. It is often added to the Iranian *coucou sabzi* recipe on page 49 and to *gormeh sabzi*, a braised lamb dish with kidney beans. In Yemen and Ethiopia, it is used as a staple vegetable.

Fresh bunches of fenugreek will keep happily in a plastic bag in the vegetable drawer of the refrigerator for up to five days.

Watercress was a highly valued spring energy tonic in ancient Persia. It gives a fabulously intense color to soups and sauces, when added at the last moment and puréed just before serving. Its wonderful hot, peppery flavor is perfect used in pesto-like sauces. Watercress is a favorite vegetable in Chinese cooking—usually briefly cooked in stir-fries or on its own, blanched and tossed with sesame oil.

Sorrel grows like a weed all over Europe and western Asia. The young leaves are quite tender and flop easily when picked, but refresh very well after 20 minutes in cold water. Don't be fooled by its spinach-like appearance, the flavor is very different—with a distinct astringent lemon taste—while the color will never be bright green like spinach. Unless the leaves are used fresh in salads, sorrel will always turn khaki green when cooked.

Sorrel is famously used in soups, especially potato soups, or in salads with sliced tomatoes and good olive oil. Roll a pile of leaves into a big fat cigar and slice thinly. One of the classic uses is in a sauce for salmon, where its acidity cuts the richness of the creamy pink flesh.

CHOOSING, CHOPPING, PRESERVING

Choosing herbs

Herbs are the best value and will have the best flavor if you buy them in big bunches from street markets and farmers' markets. Herbs bought in small packs or little pots from a supermarket may have been pampered in greenhouses and grown out of their natural season.

Herbs add their own character of flavor and fragrance on a sliding scale. Some herbs can be quite overpowering if used in a heavy-handed way, so get to know their strength.

The herb's aroma and flavor comes from the volatile oils stored in the leaves, flowers, and stems. The time of day they are harvested and the seasons can have a marked effect on their strength. The same herb grown in a variety of conditions can smell and taste quite different.

Woody herbs tend to stand up to longer cooking and can be added at the beginning of cooking. Those with soft leaves are a little more sensitive and are best added towards the end, to retain their flavor and goodness.

Chopping and preparing herbs

Herbs give out their individual aroma and flavor when chopped, torn, shredded, bruised, crushed, or heated. Useful guidelines are:

• Use a very sharp blade for chopping herbs, so the leaves don't lose all their goodness into your cutting board.
• A mezzaluna is easy to use and ideal for coarsely chopping herbs—it has a curved double-handled blade, which you rock from side to side over the leaves.
• When using a knife, wrap the herbs into a tight bunch with your fingers, then chop with the blade close to your fingers, but angled away.
• To chop even finer, bunch the leaves back together, and chop using the knife as a pivot.
• Chopping leaves in a food processor is fine if you're adding or beginning with other ingredients, otherwise I don't think it's worth it. It's much better to use a large cook's knife. If you need to use a food processor, use the pulse button to give you more control.
• Chives are easiest cut into lengths using sharp kitchen shears, unless you want a very fine finish.
• When using woody herbs or herbs with lots of stalk, strip the leaves off first.
• Herbs such as lemongrass can be bruised to bring out their maximum flavor, and used whole or thinly sliced.
• Dry leaves are better to work with, so after washing, drain well and leave on paper towels for 20 minutes to air dry. If you don't have time, don't worry—use them anyway. Stronger leaves can be dried in a salad spinner without bruising.

Preserving herbs

Once, dried herbs were almost the only preserved form we knew. Herbs grew in summer and were dried by householders for use throughout the winter and early spring. Some kept their flavor—indeed became stronger—while others faded. Modern farming methods allow us to buy many herbs at almost any time of year, but their flavor will always be different from the ones we remember in the full flush of summer. Herbs can be preserved in other ways. Cover them with olive oil—blend them with oil, let steep, strain, and use the scented oil for cooking. Freeze them and use them straight from frozen. Herbs which benefit from the cold treatment include many tropicals, such as lemongrass, kaffir lime leaves, and curry leaves. If you do use dried herbs, use a small quantity—no more than one-third of that mentioned in the recipe. Some could be left out altogether and another used instead. Use your sense of smell and taste: be creative. Remember, before cookbooks, all cooks were.

GROWING YOUR OWN

Growing your own herbs gives the best opportunity for experimenting using individual herbs and flavor combinations. Herbs are adaptable plants, generous enough to give their all, and happy to be picked continually from the garden, a terrace, or inside on a window sill. Providing you don't strip them of all greenery, herbs love to be picked. It makes them bush out and thrive in a very satisfying way. Grow the herb you use most often near the door into your garden, so it can be picked in the rain without you getting too wet. Remember, mint is the number one candidate for container growing, since it spreads like wildfire if planted in the ground and left to its own devices.

All plants grow better if their leaves are kept clean, so the kitchen is not the best place to grow herbs. The residue from all that cooking lands on the leaves and they don't respond well. So it's best to find them a bright window sill away from your cooking.

Herbs grow best organically, which has maximum benefits to our well-being, too.

The content of volatile oil stored in soft leafy herbs increases up to flowering time, when the buds have formed but are not quite open. This is when the flavor of soft leaf herbs is at its best. The best time to harvest herbs is before the sun gets too hot and after the early morning dew has dried off the leaves, so morning is good and early evening, too. As soon as they flower, you can prune them right down to get more young growth before autumn. I usually leave mine to bloom so I can make use of the flowers and also enjoy their beauty in the garden. The leaves I use will have a greater or lesser flavor over their growing season but that's what I like about herbs—they never stay the same and they're always available.

I grow herbs among ornamental shrubs and in pots. The majority of herbs adapt well to container life, although watering and feeding has to be fitted into the routine of the day, especially in the summer months. It's best to water your herbs when the sun is off the leaves.

Glazed terracotta pots hold in the moisture for longer, so keep the unglazed ones for the herbs that like the sun-baked Mediterranean conditions of a previous life.

Plants whose natural habitat is a dry rocky terrain, like thyme and rosemary, can be grown in smaller pots that may dry out faster. Choose frost-proof terracotta if you intend moving them around because they are lighter than stone. I choose not to use plastic or lead pots for health reasons.

APPETIZERS, SOUPS, AND SALADS

- **flat-leaf parsley**
- **mint (left)**

MINT AND PARSLEY SALAD
turkish ksir

½ cup bulghur wheat

2 tomatoes, halved, cored, and chopped, with the juices reserved

1 red onion or shallot, finely chopped and soaked in a little lemon juice

½ cucumber, peeled in strips, seeded, and cut into cubes

2 tablespoons extra virgin olive oil

a pinch of cayenne pepper

1 teaspoon ground sumac or the freshly squeezed juice of ½ lemon

a bunch of flat-leaf parsley

a bunch of mint

sea salt and freshly ground black pepper

lemon and lime wedges, to serve

serves 2–4

This Turkish salad of bulghur and herbs is similar to the more familiar Lebanese tabbouleh. I like the leaves coarsely chopped, with the mint chopped last, just before serving, so it doesn't turn black. Traditionally, this salad is served with pickled vegetables on boiled vine leaves. I like it served simply with lemon and lime wedges.

Put the bulghur in a bowl and cover with ⅔ cup cold water. Let stand for about 40 minutes to absorb the liquid.

Put the bulghur in a strainer and squeeze out any excess water. Transfer to a serving bowl, then add the tomatoes and their juices, onion, cucumber, olive oil, cayenne, salt, pepper, and half the sumac.

Remove the leaves from the parsley and mint and chop them coarsely. Add to the salad, toss gently, and sprinkle with the remaining sumac. Serve with lemon and lime wedges.

Cook's note The reddish-purple sumac berry is a spice tasting a little of lemons. It was used by the Romans before lemons, to do the same job. It is sold ground finely and is available from Middle Eastern stores and specialty spice markets. It's a lovely addition to this salad. If you can't find it, use the freshly squeezed juice of ½ lemon.

• savory (left)

SAVORY FETA SALAD
WITH SUGAR PEAS, EDAMAME, AND WATERMELON

8 oz. edamame (baby green soybeans)

8 oz. fava beans or peas, shelled

4 oz. sugar snap peas

½ small watermelon

¼ cup safflower oil

8 oz. feta cheese

young leaves from 5 sprigs of savory

freshly ground black pepper

serves 6

I grow winter and summer savory in my garden. They are two different plants: summer savory is an annual with tender leaves and softer stalk, while the winter version is an evergreen perennial and is a little stronger and more resinous in flavor. Both are good with beans, including edamame (baby green soybeans). Although the leaves of both summer and winter savory will toughen over the summer, they still retain a wonderful flavor. The spicy peppery taste is at its best in early summer, ready for the first crop of beans. When cut back savagely after flowering, a new crop of tender leaves will appear before fall.

Bring a large saucepan of unsalted water to a boil. Add the edamame and fava beans and blanch for 2 minutes. Drain and refresh in cold water, then remove the edamame from their pods and the fava beans from their skins.

Blanch the sugar snap peas in boiling salted water for 30 seconds, drain, refresh under cold running water, drain again, then slice lengthwise. Put in a serving bowl with the edamame and fava beans.

Peel and slice the watermelon over a bowl to catch the juices. Cut the watermelon into small wedges, as shown, and add to the bowl. Squeeze a few pieces to get about 3 tablespoons of juice in a separate bowl. Whisk the oil into the watermelon juice, then pour over the salad.

Crumble the feta over the top, sprinkle with young savory leaves and pepper, then serve.

- chervil
- young flat-leaf parsley (left)
- watercress

OYSTERS ROCKEFELLER

1 shallot, finely chopped

1 small garlic clove, crushed

1 small piece of fennel, finely chopped

6 tablespoons unsalted butter

½ cup heavy cream

3 sprigs of flat-leaf parsley

4 sprigs of chervil

4 sprigs of watercress

2 teaspoons Pernod

24 fresh oysters in the shell

a large pinch of cayenne pepper

⅓ cup fresh bread crumbs

6 tablespoons freshly
grated Parmesan cheese

sea salt and freshly ground black pepper

a broiler pan, lined with foil

serves 6

Serve this with champagne as a neat solution for a dinner party appetizer. Yes the chervil, parsley, and watercress are all important to the finished flavor, so do use them all. It's a taste revelation with the chilled oyster holding its own beneath the hot topping. You will notice that chervil not only tastes of anise, but is reminiscent of the liqueur flavor of Pernod. The original recipe was a secret, but I have added cayenne because I have a passion for it. It is just one adaptation that's been made over the years since this dish was first invented in the 1890s in New Orleans.

Put the shallot, garlic, fennel, and butter in a skillet, heat gently, and cook until softened and translucent. Add the cream and simmer for 2 minutes. Remove from the heat.

Remove the leaves from the sprigs of parsley, chervil, and watercress. Chop the leaves and add to the pan, then add the Pernod.

Shuck the oysters. Loosen each oyster from both sides of its shell with a knife and leave it in the deepest shell. Arrange the flat shells on the foil-lined broiler pan and balance the round shells on top. Put 1 teaspoon of the herb mixture on top of each oyster.

Put the cayenne, bread crumbs, Parmesan, salt, and pepper in a bowl and stir well. Put 1 teaspoon of the herb mixture on top of each oyster. Cook under a hot broiler until golden, 30–60 seconds, then serve immediately—the idea is not to cook the oysters but to maintain a hot-cold contrast.

BASIL MAYONNAISE
WITH CRISPY SHRIMP

4 oz. rice stick noodles, broken into 3

24 medium uncooked shrimp, shelled, deveined, and tail shells intact

2 sheets of nori seaweed, cut into 24 strips

peanut or safflower oil, for deep-frying

mayonnaise

leaves from a large bunch of basil, about 3 oz.

1 egg yolk

¼ teaspoon salt

1 tablespoon cider vinegar

⅓ cup olive oil

⅓ cup peanut or safflower oil

freshly squeezed juice of 1 lime

an electric deep-fryer (optional)

serves 4–6

There is life beyond basil and tomatoes. Basil is wonderful with seafood, and great with mayonnaise. Though spectacular, this dish is not difficult to make, because you can be quite haphazard about it. The noodles frizz up when fried, so all imperfections disappear.

To make the mayonnaise, bring a saucepan of water to a boil, add all the basil, and wilt briefly. Drain and run under cold water to cool quickly. Squeeze out as much water as possible and pat the basil dry with paper towels.

Put the basil in a blender with the egg yolk, salt, vinegar, and 1 tablespoon of oil. Blend to a purée and, with the motor running, gradually pour in the remaining oils until thick. Spoon into a bowl and add the lime juice to taste.

Fill a wok or deep-fryer one-third full with oil, or to the manufacturer's recommended level. Heat the oil to 375°F, or until a piece of noodle will puff up immediately. Bind the lengths of noodle onto the shrimp using a strip of the seaweed—dampen the ends of the seaweed and seal together. Add, in batches, to the hot oil and fry until they puff up and turn slightly golden, about 1 minute. Drain on paper towels and trim the ends of shrimp neatly. Serve with the mayonnaise as a dip.

Cook's extra Use the mayo with other things, such as big, homemade fries with masses of fried basil leaves.

- mint or Thai mint
- Thai sweet basil
- lemongrass
- kaffir lime leaves

THAI SPICY SQUID SALAD
yam pla muek

1½ lb. fresh squid tubes, with tentacles

¼ cup pink Thai shallots

1 stalk of lemongrass, trimmed and finely sliced

2 long red chiles, seeded and finely sliced

3 kaffir lime leaves, rolled up and finely sliced

1 inch fresh ginger, peeled, finely sliced, then cut into thin matchsticks

3 scallions, sliced diagonally

dressing

2 garlic cloves, crushed

2 medium red chiles, finely chopped

freshly squeezed juice of 4 small limes

¼ cup fish sauce

to serve

2 tablespoons chopped mint or Thai mint

a handful of Thai sweet basil leaves

serves 6

This spicy Thai squid salad is one of my favorite summer appetizers, full of light and interesting flavors—all you need to titillate the palate for the dishes to follow. If Thai mint is available, do use it. Though its fragrant leaves look a little ragged, they taste simply fabulous when chopped, adding a hotness that's certainly not to be missed. Thai mint and basil are available in bunches in Asian and Southeast Asian markets, and plants are sold in some specialty herb nurseries for you to grow in your garden. Remember they come from a hot climate, so keep them out of the frost.

To make the dressing, pound the garlic and chiles with a mortar and pestle, then add the lime juice and fish sauce. Transfer to a serving bowl and chill until needed.

Cut the squid tubes down one edge to make 1 large piece, then score the inside with a diamond pattern and cut each piece diagonally in half.

Prepare a saucepan of boiling salted water and drop the squid in the water in 2 batches. As soon as they curl up, time 1 minute, then drain immediately. Make sure to bring the water back to a boil again before dropping in the next batch. Add the squid to the chilled dressing in the serving dish while still hot.

Add the shallots, lemongrass, chiles, lime leaves, ginger, and scallions and toss gently. Top with the chopped mint and whole sweet Thai basil leaves, and serve.

shiso (perilla)

SMOKED SALMON TARTARE
WITH SHISO, WASABI JELLY, AND SALMON CAVIAR

2 tablespoons agar-agar flakes*

3 tablespoons wasabi paste

6 oz. smoked salmon

6 oz. daikon (white radish)

4 oz. jar salmon caviar (keta)

24 shiso leaves

serves 6

Agar-agar, made from seaweed, is available in Asian or natural food stores. It is popular in Asia because it sets at 99°F, so doesn't have to be refrigerated. If using other forms of agar-agar, or for vegetarian gelatin, follow the directions on the package.

Shiso leaves are the quintessential Japanese herb, sold in little trays in Japanese and Asian markets. It was also popular in Europe in Victorian times, where it was known as perilla and grown in flower beds, appreciated for its pretty, frilly leaves. I have used the green variety here—there is also a purple shiso, often known as the beefsteak plant because of the color. To my mind, shiso is sophisticated flavor heaven: the taste is highly aromatic, with warm overtones of sweet anise, cilantro, and mint. It combines perfectly with rich oily fish.

Put 1¼ cups cold water in a small saucepan. Sprinkle the agar-agar flakes over the surface and, without stirring, heat to a gentle simmer. When simmering, stir gently for 2–3 minutes. Remove the saucepan from the heat and add the wasabi, a little at a time, and mix until smooth. Pour into a shallow container, let cool, then refrigerate.

Cut the smoked salmon into small cubes. Cut the jelly into slightly smaller cubes. Peel and slice the daikon into fine matchsticks with a mandolin.

To serve, make little piles of salmon, jelly, daikon, salmon caviar, and shiso leaves.

- thyme
- marjoram
- sweet cicely or chervil (left)

CHICKEN LIVER MOUSSE

1½ sticks unsalted butter

1 garlic clove, crushed

leaves from 5 sprigs of thyme or lemon thyme

1 lb. chicken livers, trimmed

⅓ cup dry Marsala wine

leaves from 3 sprigs of marjoram

sea salt and freshly ground black pepper

sweet cicely leaves and flowers or chervil, to serve

1 bowl or 6 small ramekins

serves 6

I like the Italian flavor of Marsala instead of French brandy. The top of the pâté can be decorated with sweet cicely leaves and flowers. If these aren't available, use chervil or fine flat-leaf parsley leaves with a few pink peppercorns instead. This is great to take on a picnic, or as a appetizer for a dinner party—I serve it with toasted wafer-thin slices of walnut bread.

Heat a skillet over medium heat and add about 1 tablespoon of the butter, the garlic, half the thyme, and half the chicken livers. Cook the livers for about 1½ minutes on each side—they should still be slightly pink inside.

Transfer to a food processor and cook the remaining livers and thyme in the same way. Deglaze the pan with the Marsala, then add to the food processor. Add the marjoram leaves and 3 tablespoons of the remaining butter, a little salt, and black pepper.

Blend until smooth, then transfer to a sieve set over a bowl and push the mixture through the sieve with the back of a ladle.

Spoon the resulting mousse into the serving bowl or ramekins and tap gently on the work surface to settle the mixture. Melt the remaining butter in a small saucepan and pour over the mousse, leaving the sediment in the bottom of the pan. Arrange the sweet cicely and flowers if you have them on top and chill until needed. The mousse will keep for several days in the refrigerator.

- basil
- flat-leaf parsley
- marjoram
- Chinese flowering chives (kuchai)
- tarragon

HERB AND CARROT SOUP

3 thin leeks, finely sliced

2 garlic cloves, crushed

1 tablespoon peanut or safflower oil

1¼ lb. young carrots, well scrubbed and finely sliced

1¼ quarts vegetable stock or water

1 cup sorrel leaves, stalks removed and leaves chopped

leaves from 4 sprigs of tarragon

leaves from 6 sprigs of parsley

leaves from 4 sprigs of basil

leaves from 6 sprigs of marjoram

to serve

½ cup crème fraîche or sour cream

12 bocconcini, torn in half, or 8 oz. mozzarella cheese, torn into pieces

a handful of Chinese flowering chives (kuchai), or regular chives

freshly ground black pepper

serves 6

Aromatherapy in a soup—this dish tastes marvelous, and if you manage to grow all the ingredients yourself, you'll feel wonderfully virtuous. Purée it coarsely, so the brilliant carrot orange is just flecked with green. The bocconcini—little mouthfuls of mozzarella—peep out from just under the surface. Sprinkle with Chinese flowering chives if you have them, otherwise regular chives will taste good, too.

Put the leeks, garlic, and oil in a small saucepan, cover with a lid, and cook gently for 5 minutes. Add the carrots and cook gently for a further 5 minutes. Add the stock, bring to a boil, and simmer for 5 minutes. Lower the heat, add the sorrel, and simmer, uncovered, for a further 5 minutes.

Coarsely chop the tarragon, parsley, basil, and marjoram. Stir into the pan. Strain the mixture through a sieve into a clean pan and put the solids into a food processor with a little of the liquid. Blend to a coarse purée, then return to the pan and reheat.

Remove from the heat, fold in the crème fraîche. Ladle into hot bowls and add a few bocconcini pieces to each one, then serve sprinkled with chive flowers and pepper.

• chervil (left)
• watercress

SOUPE VERDON

1 large onion, finely chopped

1 tablespoon peanut or safflower oil

1 small potato, about 4 oz., chopped

1 Golden Delicious apple,
peeled and finely chopped

1 quart vegetable or light chicken broth

a large bunch of watercress

a handful of chervil

sea salt and freshly ground white pepper

to serve

heavy cream or crème fraîche

avruga or other caviar (optional)

serves 4–6

This bright green soup is named after the beautiful river in Provence, north of Brignoles—the green minerals in the rocky bed make the water a wonderful color. I like it served hot, but it makes a lovely change to have it cold—you will get maximum color, flavor, and goodness if you blend the herbs into the chilled soup.

Put the onion and oil in a saucepan, heat gently, then cook for 5 minutes until softened and translucent. Add the potato and apple, cover with a lid, and continue cooking gently for a further 5 minutes. Add the broth and bring to a boil, lower the heat, and simmer for 10 minutes.

Remove any thick or tough stalks from the watercress and remove the chervil stalks (which can taste over-grassy). Chop the watercress and chervil leaves and add to the soup. Simmer for 1 minute, then strain into a clean saucepan. Put the solids from the strainer into a blender with a little of the liquid and blend to a purée. Return to the pan and reheat gently.

Serve with a swirl of cream or crème fraîche and a spoonful of caviar.

- kaffir lime leaves
- Thai sweet basil
- garlic chives (flat Chinese chives)

THAI LOBSTER NOODLE SOUP

2 small cooked lobsters
or crayfish tails, shells removed

4 oz. dried shrimp

3 kaffir lime leaves, torn

1 inch fresh ginger, peeled

8 oz. wide rice noodles (sen lek)

2 tablespoons hijiki seaweed

2 tablespoons mirin (sweetened
Japanese rice wine)

¾ cup coconut cream

2 tablespoons fish sauce

freshly squeezed juice of 1 lime

2 mild red chiles, halved lengthwise,
seeded, and finely sliced

2 mild green chiles, seeded
and finely sliced into thin strips

a handful of garlic chives, sliced diagonally

½ cup thin green beans, sliced in half
lengthwise and cooked

2 sprigs of sweet Thai basil

serves 4

Like so much Thai food, this recipe has a delicate balance of spicy, fresh, zesty flavors. Kaffir lime leaves are increasingly available, either as part of a Thai flavor package in supermarkets, or in bags from Asian or Chinatown markets. Buy the whole bag and freeze them, then use straight from frozen. Ginger can also be frozen, then grated from frozen. Both flavors contrast well with the richness of coconut milk and lobster. Seaweed or sesame seeds are my own additions—less Thai than Japanese, but no less delicious for all that.

Put the lobster shells, dried shrimp, and kaffir lime leaves in a large saucepan. Add 1½ quarts water and bring to a boil, then reduce the heat and simmer for 1 hour. Strain the broth. Grate the ginger, and squeeze the juice from it into the broth.

Soak the noodles in a bowl of cold water for 20 minutes. When soft, drain well and cover until needed. Put the seaweed in a bowl and stir in the mirin.

Add the coconut cream to the broth, stir well, and bring to a boil. Lower the heat, then add fish sauce and lime juice to taste.

When ready to serve, add the drained noodles to the broth and reheat. Ladle into hot bowls, then add the chiles, chives, beans, and lobster meat. Drain the seaweed and sprinkle it over the soup, then top with Thai sweet basil leaves, and serve.

Cook's extra Fishsellers and Chinese supermarkets often have frozen crayfish tails, which are good for this recipe. Instead of hijiki seaweed, I sometimes use black sesame seeds to sprinkle on top.

BRUNCHES AND LIGHT LUNCHES

- **pandanus**
- **sorrel (left)**
- **flat-leaf parsley**

SORREL-SPINACH SOUFFLÉS IN PANDAN LEAVES

Sorrel can sometimes be bought in produce stores or farmers' markets, but otherwise grows easily in the garden. When heated, it turns khaki, unlike spinach, which just becomes a more brilliant green. The pandanus leaves used to wrap the soufflés can be found in Asian stores, and give delicate scent and flavor. Don't worry if you can't find them (just omit)—but if you do, it's always exciting to try new things.

14 pandanus leaves (pandan or screwpine), about 18 inches long (optional)

softened unsalted butter, for greasing

⅔ cup milk

⅔ cup heavy cream

1½ cups torn spinach

½ cup sorrel leaves

leaves from 4 sprigs of flat-leaf parsley, chopped

2 tablespoons unsalted butter

3 tablespoons all-purpose flour

8 oz. soft goat cheese, such as chèvre blanc

4 egg yolks

5 egg whites

sea salt and freshly ground black pepper

4 ramekins, about 1 cup each, buttered and chilled

serves 4

If using pandanus leaves, trim both ends to a point. Rub the central 7 inches of 12 of the leaves (shiny side) with butter. Line each ramekin with 3 leaves, buttered side downward, so the ends stand upright above the rim of the ramekin.

Cut the remaining 2 pandanus leaves into pieces and put in a saucepan. Add the milk and cream and warm to just below boiling point. Remove from the heat and set aside to infuse.

Plunge the spinach and sorrel into a saucepan of boiling water for 20 seconds, then drain and refresh in cold water. Drain well and squeeze out every drop of water (I squeeze them in cheesecloth). Chop coarsely, add the parsley, and reserve until required.

Melt the butter in a small saucepan, stir in the flour, let cook for 1 minute, then strain in the milk and cream and beat until thickened. Crumble the cheese into the sauce and season well with salt and pepper.

Purée the spinach, sorrel, sauce, and egg yolks in a blender, then transfer to a bowl. Put the egg whites in a second bowl and beat until soft peaks form. Fold into the sorrel mixture, a little at first to loosen, then fold in gently so as not to lose any volume. Carefully spoon the mixture into the ramekins to within ½ inch of the rims. At this point, they can be kept on a tray in the refrigerator for up to 2 hours. When ready to serve, cook on the lowest shelf of a preheated oven at 375°F for 25–30 minutes until risen and golden. Remove from the oven and let stand for a few minutes until the sides shrink slightly. Lift the soufflés out of the ramekins, set gently on warm plates, and serve immediately.

GRILLED CHILE HERB POLENTA
WITH PAPAYA MOJO

a handful of chives

a small bunch of cilantro

4 sprigs of oregano

1½ cups quick-cook polenta or cornmeal

4 tablespoons unsalted butter, cut into pieces

⅔ cup Asiago vecchio cheese, freshly grated

2 long red chiles, seeded and finely chopped

olive oil spray

sea salt and freshly ground black pepper

papaya mojo

2–3 small pink Thai shallots, finely sliced

grated zest and freshly squeezed juice of 1 lime

5 tablespoons olive oil

1 large papaya, peeled and cut into cubes

a handful of chives, chopped

a small bunch of cilantro

sea salt and freshly ground black pepper

epazote beans

½ cup black beans, rinsed and drained

2 sprigs of epazote or a pinch of dried

*a baking dish,
about 9 x 12 cm, oiled*

serves 6

Epazote is a Mexican herb, available fresh and dried in Latino markets. It grows like a weed in the garden, and sprouted every year in all my flower pots, until one year it suddenly disappeared. I found I really missed its skunk-like, pungent aroma. Kate, our photographer's assistant, thinks it smells very clean—like bleach. It is famous as a partner for beans, because it counteracts their gaseous tendencies.

To prepare the beans, put them in a bowl, cover with cold water, and let soak overnight. Drain, rinse, and put them in a saucepan. Cover again with cold water and bring to a boil for 5 minutes. Lower the heat, add the epazote, and simmer until just cooked—about 1 hour.

Put the chives, cilantro, and oregano leaves on a board and chop them coarsely. Bring 1 quart water to a boil and add a pinch of salt. Add the polenta or cornmeal all at once, beating constantly. As it thickens, stir in the butter and cheese. Mix well, then fold in the herbs, chiles, salt, and pepper.

Pour into the oiled baking dish, smooth the top with a spatula, and let cool. Leave uncovered and let chill for 30 minutes before finishing.

To make the mojo, put the shallots, and lime juice in a bowl, stir gently, then gradually stir in the oil, papaya, salt, and pepper. Add the cilantro leaves and bean mixture and fold in.

Carefully take the polenta out of the pan and put on a board. Cut into 12 wedges. Heat a ridged stove-top grill pan and, when it starts to smoke, lower the heat a little, spray with olive oil, and add the polenta wedges. Grill on the top side for 2 minutes, then turn the pieces 180 degrees to create a criss-cross pattern. Cook another minute. Serve hot with the papaya mojo and beans.

- chervil
- tarragon (left)
- chives or Chinese chives

BAKED RICOTTA AND HERB TERRINE

1 cup fresh ricotta cheese

4 eggs

1 egg yolk

2 tablespoons all-purpose flour

⅔ cup freshly grated pecorino cheese

½ teaspoon coarsely crushed dried green peppercorns

a small bunch of chervil

a small bunch of tarragon

a small bunch of chives, with flowers if possible

to serve

herb oil

herb leaf salad

3 tomatoes, preferably an heirloom variety such as Green Zebra

a loaf pan, 8 x 4 inches, greased with butter

a roasting pan or similar dish, to hold the loaf pan

serves 6

I make this terrine in summer with herbs straight from the garden. If the chives are in flower, pluck the petals apart and sprinkle them over each serving. Serve with accompaniments such as the full-flavored heirloom tomatoes you find in specialist produce stores and farmers' markets. This one is called Green Zebra.

Put the ricotta in a bowl and beat with a wooden spoon until smooth. Beat in the eggs and egg yolk, one at a time. Put the flour, pecorino, and pepper in a bowl, stir well, then beat into the ricotta mixture.

Reserve a few chives leaves, then coarsely chop the remaining chives, chervil, and tarragon. Fold them into the ricotta. Spoon the mixture into the prepared loaf pan, stand it in a roasting pan and fill with enough water to come halfway up the outside of the loaf pan. (This is called a bain-marie or water bath.) Bake uncovered in a preheated oven at 350°F for 35–45 minutes until risen, golden, and set.

Remove from the roasting pan (as the terrine cools it will shrink away from the sides a little). After about 8 minutes, run a knife around the sides of the terrine, then carefully invert it onto a serving dish or board. Slice and serve or, if serving cold, let cool for at least 15 minutes.

Cook's note Pecorino is a sheep's milk cheese, stronger than Parmesan (which could be used instead).

- parsley
- mint
- oregano
- fennel

HERB OMELET WITH SHRIMP
coucou sabzi

6–8 uncooked peeled shrimp, tail fins on

6 large eggs

5 tablespoons olive oil

½ cup milk

1 small bulb of fennel, finely sliced, then chopped, and a large handful of the green leaves

3 scallions, finely sliced

1 young leek, finely sliced

4 sprigs of parsley

4 sprigs of mint

a small handful of oregano leaves

a large handful of fennel fronds

sea salt and freshly ground black pepper

to serve

crusty bread

crisp green salad

an ovenproof dish, 8 x 11 inches, preferably nonstick, oiled

serves 6

Iran (Persia) boasts one of the world's great cuisines, and *coucou sabzi* (a herb omelet) is one of its best-known dishes. I have added chunky shrimp to make it a more substantial lunch dish. If you don't have a suitable oven dish, use a skillet with an ovenproof handle to finish off the cooking. Fennel leaves are quite hard to find in stores, because they wilt easily. If you don't grow it yourself, use the green sprouting tops from bulb fennel instead.

To prepare the shrimp, devein them, then "butterfly" them—cut down the back lengthwise, but leave the tail fins intact, so they will sit upright when cooked.

Put the eggs in a bowl, add salt and pepper and 2 tablespoons of the olive oil. Beat briefly with a fork or whisk.

Put 2 tablespoons of the olive oil in a skillet, heat gently, then add the chopped fennel and wilt for about 3 minutes. Add the scallions and leek and stir to wilt a little. Stir into the bowl of eggs.

Put the leaves of parsley, mint, oregano, and half the fennel fronds on a board. Chop them all together, then stir into the eggs. Pour into the prepared ovenproof dish, then sit the shrimp upright in the dish.

Cover carefully with foil and cook in a preheated oven at 350°F for 25 minutes, then uncover and continue baking until cooked and golden. Tear the remaining fennel fronds over the top. Set aside for a few minutes before serving.

Cut into wedges, including at least 1 shrimp in each piece. Sprinkle with extra herbs and serve with crusty bread and a crisp green salad.

FILIPINO MARINATED FISH SALAD WITH CHIVES
kilaw

3 fillets of fine-textured fish with red, pink, or silver skins, such as snapper or sea bass, about 1½ lb.

freshly squeezed juice of 2 limes

freshly squeezed juice of 2 lemons

2 pink Thai shallots or 1 regular shallot, halved and finely sliced

1 inch fresh ginger, peeled and finely sliced into thin matchsticks

¾ cup coconut cream

1 green serrano chile, seeded and thinly sliced

1 red serrano chile, seeded and thinly sliced

6 scallions, finely sliced

a small handful of cilantro

6 sprigs of Chinese flowering chives (kuchai)

6 lime wedges, to serve

serves 6

This marinated fish salad from the Philippines uses the same technique of "cooking" fish in lime juice as the Latin American dish seviche—the acid in the juice changes the texture of the fish and the flesh becomes opaque. Chinese flowering chives, also known as kuchai, are sold in Chinese markets. The leaves are flat, while the flowering stems are round, not hollow, like regular chives. The buds should be closed—if they're open, they're past their best. However, I like to use the flowers to decorate this dish—they have quite a chunky stalk and can be snipped straight into the dish exactly like chives. If you can't find them, use regular chives and a small garlic clove, crushed.

Cut the fish crosswise into 2-inch pieces and put into a non-metallic dish. Pour over the lime and lemon juices and sprinkle with the shallots and ginger. Cover with plastic wrap and set aside for 4 hours in the refrigerator. Drain the juices from the fish and mix the juices with the coconut cream.

Arrange the fish in a serving dish, pour over the coconut cream mixture, and top with the chiles, scallions, cilantro, and Chinese flowering chives. Serve the lime wedges separately.

• dill (left)

2 lb. salmon fillet

2 tablespoons gin

a large bunch of dill

5 tablespoons sea salt flakes

3 tablespoons sugar

pancakes

¾ cup self-rising flour

a pinch of salt

¼ teaspoon baking powder

1 egg

1 teaspoon Dijon mustard

¾ cup milk

1 tablespoon freshly chopped dill leaves

peanut or safflower oil, for cooking

sabayon

2 egg yolks

1 tablespoon thin honey

2 tablespoons Dijon mustard

3 tablespoons gin

*a poffertje or aebelskiver pan,
blini pan, or crêpe pan*

**serves 6–8:
makes about 36 pancakes**

DILL-MARINATED SALMON
WITH PANCAKES AND SABAYON

This traditionally cured salmon takes 36–48 hours to cure and the flavor of the dill penetrates right into the fish. I use a whole fillet of salmon for a party, but if you want it for a smaller group, just halve the recipe. My neighbour, Ireen, is Dutch and she lends me a special pan, called a *poffertjes* pan, with 19 indentations in it so the little pancakes can be cooked in large batches. Instead, you can use a doughnut pan, such as *aebleskiver* or blini pan, or make tiny ones, a few at a time, in a regular crêpe pan. A flavored sabayon is served instead of the usual dill and mustard sauce.

Put the fish on a board, flesh side up, and rub with the gin. Remove the dill fronds from the thick stalks, chop them, mix with the salt and sugar, and rub into the flesh. Put in a non-metallic dish and cover with plastic wrap. Put a board on top with weights on top of that (2 heavy food cans are suitable). Chill for 36–48 hours. Slice thinly at a 45 degree angle to serve.

To make the pancake batter, sift the flour, salt, and baking powder into a bowl. Make a hollow in the middle, add the egg, mustard, and half the milk. Beat gently, then slowly add the rest of the milk to make a smooth batter. Add the chopped dill and beat into the mixture.

Lightly oil the chosen pan. Heat the pan and fill each indentation with batter almost to the top. Sauté them until their undersides are brown, then flip them and cook the other side. Keep warm while the remaining batter is cooked.

Just before serving, make the sabayon sauce. Put the egg yolks, honey, mustard, and gin in a bowl set over a saucepan of barely simmering water so the bowl doesn't touch the water. Using a hand-held electric beater, beat until the volume has increased and the mixture is foaming and holding its shape.

Serve the pancakes topped with a slice of salmon and a spoonful of sabayon.

A MEAL IN A PAN

10 oz. medium new potatoes

2 tablespoons olive oil

1 tablespoon salted butter

4 oz. smoked salmon

a small bunch of dill
(strip the feathery leaves
from any very thick stalks)

2 eggs

sea salt and freshly ground pepper,
pink or black

*2 small skillets, about 6 inches diameter,
or 1 medium skillet*

serves 2

The delicate fern-like glamour of dill is best when fresh, with upright, bright green fronds and umbrellas of pin-like bright yellow flowers. Dill and fennel are famous digestive aids, and are often added to dishes perceived as very rich or fatty, or difficult-to-digest ingredients such as pickled cucumbers or cabbage. In this recipe, dill calms the richness of smoked salmon and egg.

Put the potatoes in a large saucepan, add cold water to cover, bring to a boil, add a large pinch of salt, and cook until tender. Drain and, when cool enough to handle, peel or not, as you wish. Slice into ¼-inch rounds.

Heat the pan or pans. Add 1 tablespoon of oil and a piece of butter to each pan. As soon as it sizzles, add the sliced potatoes. Sauté on both sides over medium heat until golden.

Divide the smoked salmon between the pans, folding it over the potatoes. Tear the dill over the top and break an egg into the center of each pan. Add the pepper, cover with a plate or lid, and cook over low heat for 3 minutes until the egg has just set.

Cook's extra Scallops can be used instead of the salmon. Slice crosswise into disks and sauté briefly.

- **flat-leaf parsley (left)**
- **bay leaves**
- **thyme**

PARSLEYED HAM
jambon persillé

2 lb. best-quality cured pork or ham steak,
soaked overnight

1 medium veal knuckle, chopped into pieces

1 shallot

2 carrots

¼ teaspoon black peppercorns

a large bunch of flat-leaf parsley

2 bay leaves

a large sprig of thyme

4 sheets of leaf gelatin or 15 g powder
(optional)

⅔ cup white wine

1 tablespoon tarragon vinegar

3 egg whites and shells

serves 6–8

This Burgundian Easter classic requires lots of very fresh flat-leaf
parsley and a beautiful piece of cured ham, plus some jelly-making
ingredients and a large pinch of commitment!

Put the pork or ham, veal, shallot, carrots, and peppercorns in a large saucepan.
Strip the leaves off the parsley and put them in a plastic bag in the refrigerator.
Tie up the parsley stalks, bay leaves, and thyme with twine to make a bouquet
garni and add to the pan. Cover with water and heat to a gentle simmer with
the water hardly moving. Cook for about 1½ hours or until very tender.

Lift the ham out onto a plate and let cool. When cold, cover and store in the
refrigerator. Simmer the liquid for another 30 minutes. Lift out the knuckle and
strain the liquid through a sieve into a bowl and let cool. When cool, measure
3 cups and put it in the refrigerator overnight (keep the rest for soup).

If it has set to a firm jelly, there will be no need to use the gelatin (otherwise
soak and use the gelatin after clarifying the liquid). If it has not set, use a baster
to extract liquid from the center, leaving the fat behind. If it has set, skim off any
fat and spoon the jelly into a saucepan. Heat until just melted. Add the wine
and vinegar.

Put the egg whites and shells in a bowl and beat well. Add to the pan and,
beating constantly, gradually bring to a boil. As soon as the froth rises to the
top of the pan, stop beating and take it off the heat. Let settle for 4 minutes.

Take care that the crust on top does not break, then heat the liquid once again
just to a boil. As soon as it rises, take off the heat and leave for 10 minutes.

Meanwhile cut the ham into small pieces discard any fat. Gently strain the liquid
through a sieve set over a bowl lined with a double thickness of cheesecloth.
Cool to a point where it has almost set to jelly. Chop the reserved parsley
leaves and add to the jelly. Then add the ham. Spoon into a glass bowl right to
the top (or use several small bowls), then let set in the refrigerator.

- **kaffir lime leaves**
- **Thai holy basil**

THAI BEEF CURRY WITH BASIL
pha naeng neua

1½ lb. beef tenderloin

1¾ cups coconut milk

1–2 tablespoons red Thai curry paste

⅔ cup peanuts, roasted and ground

2 tablespoons palm sugar or brown sugar

5 kaffir lime leaves

3 tablespoons fish sauce

a bunch of Thai holy basil

freshly squeezed juice of ½ lime,
or to taste

to serve

2 teaspoons peanut or safflower oil

1½ cups bean sprouts,
rinsed, trimmed, and drained

8 Thai shallots or 2 regular shallots,
finely sliced

2 mild green chiles, seeded and
sliced into rings (optional)

serves 6

There are two kinds of Thai holy basil—the one with dark purple-tinged leaf, stalk, and flower is the most fragrant when heated in curries, and this one is the variety used in meat curries. The leaves are more sturdy and, when you crush them between your fingers, they have a minty, almost camphor-like aroma. The lighter, paler, Thai holy basil has a softer, slightly hairy leaf with a distinct oily aroma. It is used in non-meat curries and noodle dishes. If you can't find either of these, sprinkle Thai sweet basil over the dish at the last moment.

Cut the beef in half lengthwise, then into thin diagonal slices. Put half the coconut milk and all the red curry paste in a wok and heat slowly until just boiling. Add the rest of the milk and simmer gently for 5 minutes. Add the peanuts, palm sugar, and kaffir lime leaves and simmer for a further 2 minutes. Strip the leaves from the holy basil and add to the wok, then add the fish sauce. Stir in the beef and cook for 1 minute to wilt the leaves and lightly cook the beef. Add lime juice to taste and serve in 6 deep bowls.

Heat the oil in a wok, add the bean sprouts, and stir-fry for 1 minute. Serve in bowls topped with the shallots and chiles, if using.

Cook's extra To seed a chile before slicing into rings, massage it between your thumb and forefinger until it feels loose inside. Cut off the stalk end and bang the chile on the work surface so all the seeds fall out. To cut into fine matchsticks, cut in half lengthwise and remove the seeds with a teaspoon. Slice finely.

ENTRÉES

● **fennel**

FISH IN FENNEL SALT CRUST

2 lemons

a 2-lb. red snapper or sea bass,
scaled and cleaned

plenty of fennel stalks, foliage, and flowers

8 oz. grey sea salt

8 oz. kosher salt

serves 2

I grow two kinds of fennel in my garden—regular and bronze. It's a pretty herb to grow, but if you don't have any, use the tops from a bulb of Florence fennel. However, in this recipe I like to use the whole plant—stalks, foliage, and flowers. The salt forms a crust which keeps the fish moist. It does not make the fish very salty, because the crust is removed before serving, but it does somehow enhance the flavor of the sea. Use all kosher salt if necessary.

Cut 1 lemon into slices and use to stuff the cavity of the fish. Reserve a handful of fennel, and stuff the rest into the cavity.

Put the two kinds of salt in a bowl and mix well. Put half the mixture in an ovenproof dish and shake to level. Arrange the fish in a single layer, then pack the remaining salt over the fish. Insert the remaining fennel into the salt.

Bake in a preheated oven at 400°F for 15–20 minutes or until done. To test, insert a skewer through the salt into the fish—if it comes out very hot, the fish is done.

Crack open the crust and remove most of the salt. Serve with the rest of the lemon cut into wedges.

Cook's extra Serve with a simple salsa of tomato, parsley, and onions, all chopped finely and mixed with olive oil.

- cilantro
- mint

FISH WITH CILANTRO AND MINT WRAPPED IN LEAVES
patra ni macchi

6 skinless halibut fillets about 6–8 oz. each

freshly squeezed juice of 1 lime,
plus 1 lime, cut into wedges, to serve

sea salt

6 patra leaves or 6 pieces of banana leaf
or foil, about 9 inches square

cilantro mint chutney

⅔ cup unsweetened dried shredded coconut

3 garlic cloves, crushed

3 large green chiles,
seeded and finely chopped

a large bunch of cilantro

a large bunch of mint

½ teaspoon sugar

½ teaspoon ground coriander

freshly squeezed juice of 1 lime

sea salt

raffia or string, to tie the packages

serves 6

Real chutney, in India, is fresh, and quite unlike Western versions. This one is flavored with spices as well as cilantro and mint and is bright green, in terrific contrast to the white flesh of the fish. Patra, traditionally used to wrap the fish, is taro leaf, sold in Asian markets. If you can't find it, use banana leaves instead—or just foil. Either way, the package is unwrapped before eating—you don't eat the wrapper.

Put the fish on a plate. Mix the lime juice with the salt and rub into the fish. Cover and set aside in a cool place.

To make the chutney, put the coconut, garlic, chiles, cilantro leaves, mint, sugar, ground coriander, lime juice, and a small pinch of salt in a food processor and pulse to a coarse paste.

Use the paste to coat the topside and underside of the fish, then wrap in leaves or foil and tie with raffia or twine.

Arrange the fish packages on a rack in a baking dish with a little boiling water in the bottom. Cover with a foil tent and cook in a preheated oven at 425°F for about 15–20 minutes.

- **flat-leaf parsley**
- **cilantro**

HAKE IN GREEN SAUCE

12 mussels

16 clams

½ cup cava sparkling wine

4 hake steaks cut through the bone, about
8 oz. each (leave the bone in)

⅔ cup olive oil

4 garlic cloves, thinly sliced

1 tablespoon finely chopped parsley,
plus sprigs to serve

1 tablespoon finely chopped cilantro leaves

sea salt

serves 4

Hake is a favorite fish in Spain, where I discovered this dish. It is becoming seriously overfished, so feel free to substitute other white fish, such as pollock, or haddock. As it cooks, the fish gives out white juices, which you shake to form an emulsion with the oil. Wine and chopped herbs turn this emulsion into a wonderfully delicious green sauce. This dish is usually cooked in a flameproof earthenware cazuela, a flat cooking dish that retains heat well. I find a heavy enameled nonstick skillet works well, too.

Put the mussels, clams, and wine in a saucepan over high heat. As the shellfish open, remove them to a bowl, and cover with plastic wrap. Discard any that don't open. Pour the cooking juices through a cheesecloth-lined strainer and set aside.

Put the hake on a plate and sprinkle with a little salt 10 minutes before cooking.

Put the oil and garlic in a heavy skillet and heat gently so the garlic turns golden slowly and doesn't burn. Remove the garlic with a slotted spoon and set aside until ready to serve.

Pour about two-thirds of the oil into a measuring cup and add the hake to the oil left in the pan. Cook over very low heat, moving the pan in a circular motion—keep taking it off the heat so it doesn't cook too quickly (the idea is to encourage the oozing of the juices instead of letting them sauté and burn). Add the remaining oil little by little as you move the pan, so an emulsion starts to form. When all the oil has been added, remove the fish to a plate and keep it warm. Put the pan on the heat, add the reserved clam juices, and stir to form the sauce.

Return the fish to the pan, add the chopped parsley and cilantro, and continue to cook until the fish is done, about 5 minutes. Just before serving, add the opened mussels, clams, and fried garlic to heat through.

- lemongrass
- kaffir lime leaves
- vietnamese cilantro (laksa leaves) (left)

FRIED SNAPPER THAI-STYLE

I encountered this idea in a tiny eatery on a remote island in Thailand. It had just three tables and food was cooked on burners set on the ground behind a rush screen. Lunch was whatever the ocean had to offer that day. The view was spiritually uplifting and the food was divine. I could no more live without the classic Thai ingredients—lemongrass and kaffir lime leaf—than garlic and onions. The lime leaf's Thai name is *makrut*—"kaffir" is the Hindi word for a foreigner, perhaps reflecting the odd way the leaves grow—in pairs. They are waxy and smooth, in contrast to the fruit, which has knobbly skin. Both leaf and zest have a wonderfully fragrant lime flavor.

8 red snapper or porgy fillets, about 1½ lb.

3 tablespoons peanut or safflower oil

3 red chiles, seeded and finely sliced

2 stalks of lemongrass, trimmed and finely sliced

8 pink Thai shallots or 2 regular shallots, finely sliced

2 inches fresh ginger, peeled, thinly sliced, and cut into matchstick strips

6 kaffir lime leaves, rolled and finely sliced

12–18 Vietnamese cilantro (laksa leaves)

oil, for frying

6 limes, cut into wedges, to serve

marinade

2 garlic cloves, finely chopped

2 stalks of lemongrass, trimmed and finely sliced

1 teaspoon coriander seeds

1 teaspoon Szechuan pepper

1 teaspoon finely ground star anise

1 teaspoon ground galangal (Laos powder)

½ teaspoon salt

½ teaspoon freshly ground black pepper

serves 4

Cut each fillet in half and slash twice on the skin side.

To make the marinade, use a mortar and pestle to grind the garlic, lemongrass, coriander seeds, Szechuan pepper, star anise, galangal, salt, and pepper to a fine paste. Rub the paste into the slashes and into the flesh side of the fish pieces, then let marinate for 30 minutes.

Meanwhile, fill a wok about one-third full with oil, heat to about 375°F, or until a piece of noodle will puff up immediately. Add the chiles, lemongrass, shallots, ginger, and lime leaves and deep-fry until crispy—work in batches if necessary to ensure a crisp result. Fry the Vietnamese cilantro separately—the leaves are left whole and are fragile when crisp. Remove from the wok and drain on paper towels. Pour the oil into a heatproof container and let cool.

To cook the fish, wipe any excess marinade off the skin side. Put about ½ cup of the oil back into the wok and heat gently. Working in batches, sauté the fish, flesh side down over medium heat, for 1 minute, then turn the pieces over and sauté for 1 minute more. As each piece is done, remove from the wok and pile onto plates. Serve topped with the crispy lemongrass mixture, deep-fried Vietnamese cilantro, and lime wedges.

- chervil
- flat-leaf parsley
- celery leaves

CRISP-FRIED HERBED HALIBUT
WITH SHOESTRING POTATOES

1½ lb. salad potatoes

1 egg white

1 tablespoon milk

1½ lb. halibut fillet, cut into 8 pieces

3 sprigs of chervil

3 sprigs of flat-leaf parsley

⅔ cup all-purpose flour

1 teaspoon black sesame seeds

½ teaspoon chile powder

sea salt and freshly ground white pepper

peanut or safflower oil, for deep-frying

to serve

celery leaves

flat-leaf parsley leaves

spicy ketchup, for dipping

an electric deep-fryer

serves 4

Celery leaf is a delicious herb, and plants are now available in pots from garden centers. You could also use the pale leaves growing inside an ordinary head of celery. Celery and flat-leaf parsley leaves are perfect crisply fried and curly parsley is also good. Chervil and parsley are used to flavor the coating on the fish.

Using a mandolin, cut the potatoes as thinly as possible into strips, then put into a bowl of cold water to rinse off the starch. Drain and dry well with paper towels.

Fill a deep-fryer with oil to the manufacturer's recommended level and heat to 350°F. Working in batches, fry the potatoes until golden, then drain on paper towels. Keep hot.

Put the egg white and milk in a bowl and mix well. Rub the fish pieces with the egg white mixture. Finely chop the leaves from the chervil and parsley.

Sift the flour into a bowl, then add the chopped chervil and parsley, the sesame seeds, chile powder, salt, and pepper.

Deep-fry the celery and parsley leaves—they spit like crazy, but will be crisp as soon as the spitting stops. Remove, and drain on paper towels. Dip the fish into the bowl of flour mixture to coat, and fry 2 pieces at a time for 2–3 minutes until just cooked. Drain on paper towels and serve with the fried leaves, ketchup, and crisp shoestring potatoes.

• chives (left)
• wild leeks (ramps)

SEA BASS WITH CHIVE CREAM

4–8 sea bass fillets

salt

oil, for brushing (optional)

chive cream

6 tablespoons unsalted butter,
cut into pieces

2 thin banana shallots or 4 regular,
finely chopped

½ cup white wine

½ cup heavy cream

a handful of chives

4 wild leek leaves (optional)

sea salt and freshly ground black pepper

to serve (optional)

caviar

wild garlic flowers

Chinese bamboo steamers

serves 4

An elegant dinner party dish—serve two fillets for an entrée or one for a fish course. The caviar is an indulgence which you can choose to have—or have not! Everyone should grow chives in a patch in the garden or in a pot on the terrace or window sill, partly because you can harvest the pinky purple pincushion flowers anytime for salads or sprinkling over dishes, but mainly because it's so nice to grab a handful of spiky leaves to snip over buttery new potatoes or mashed potatoes. If you have access to wild scallions (ramps), a few flowers will add a stylish look and the leaves add extra flavor.

To make the chive cream, put 2 tablespoons of the butter in a skillet, add the shallots, and cook for 3 minutes without coloring. Add the wine and cook until reduced by two-thirds. Add the cream and bring to a boil, remove from the heat, then beat in the remaining butter and add salt and pepper to taste.

Brush the grids of the steamers with oil, or line with 3 of the garlic leaves.

Sprinkle the flesh side of the sea bass with a little salt and fold in half with the skin on the outside. Steam in Chinese steamers over simmering water for about 2 minutes. Check to make sure the fish is still folded—if not, press down with a spoon and continue steaming for a further 2 minutes until just cooked (remember the fish will carry on cooking in its own heat, so don't overdo the cooking).

When the fish is almost done, chop the chives and one of the garlic leaves, if using. Put in a blender, pour in the cream and shallot mixture, and purée until smooth. Reheat very gently without boiling. Put 1–2 pieces of fish on each plate, with the sauce under or over it. Top with a spoonful of caviar and wild garlic flowers, if using, and serve.

CILANTRO CHICKEN WITH FENUGREEK

6 skinless, boneless chicken thighs

1 teaspoon cumin seeds, freshly ground

¼ cup peanut or safflower oil

1 onion, finely chopped

5 garlic cloves, crushed

2 inches fresh ginger, peeled and grated

4 green chiles, seeded and chopped, plus extra for serving

½ teaspoon ground turmeric

2 teaspoons coriander seeds, freshly ground

½ teaspoon fenugreek seeds, toasted in a dry skillet, then ground

1¾ cups coconut milk

leaves from a bunch of fenugreek (methi), about 1 oz., or a pinch of ground fenugreek

leaves from a bunch of fresh cilantro, plus extra sprigs, to serve

½ cup roasted slivered almonds, toasted in a dry skillet

sea salt and freshly ground black pepper

Indian breads, such as pooris, or rice, to serve

a casserole dish with a lid

serves 4

The seeds of the fenugreek or methi plant are a common Indian spice. The leaves of the plant are sold in Indian and Middle Eastern produce stores, and the spice seeds in the spice section of many supermarkets. In fact, they are what gives curry powder its distinctive aroma. In my opinion, nothing compares with the astringently aromatic flavor of the fresh leaves and, if you have a garden, it's definitely worth growing yourself. However, when you buy the leaves, make sure they are fresh and perky—don't keep them too long in water, because the leaves will lose their flavor. If you can't buy fresh fenugreek, this recipe is also good with just fresh cilantro leaves and some fenugreek seed.

Cut the chicken into large pieces, season with salt, pepper, and ground cumin and set aside for 15 minutes at room temperature to develop the flavors.

Heat 2 tablespoons of the oil in a casserole dish, add the chicken pieces, and sauté until golden. Using a slotted spoon, remove to a plate. Heat the remaining oil in the casserole, add the garlic, and sauté until softened and translucent, about 7 minutes. Add the garlic, ginger, and chiles, increase the heat, and add the turmeric, coriander, and fenugreek seeds. Stir in 1 cup of the coconut milk and heat to simmering. Return the chicken pieces to the casserole and cover with the lid. Cook in a preheated oven at 375°F for 20 minutes.

Put the fenugreek leaves and cilantro into a blender, add the remaining coconut milk, and blend to a purée. Add to the chicken and cook for a further 5–10 minutes. Top with cilantro sprigs, almonds, and extra chile, if using, and serve with Indian pooris or rice.

BREAST OF GUINEA FOWL
STUFFED WITH GOAT
CHEESE AND HYSSOP

1 tablespoon olive oil

4 guinea fowl breasts, with wing bone only left in and skin on

6 oz. firm goat cheese, rind removed

4 sprigs of hyssop or lemon thyme

2 tablespoons thick honey

6 teaspoons orange flower water or orange juice

sea salt and freshly ground black pepper

herb and flower salad, to serve

a shallow flameproof dish

serves 4

Hyssop is still used today in Bedouin cooking. A native of the Mediterranean, it has pink or blue flowers which, like all herb flowers, are pretty in salads and to sprinkle over other dishes. It has a sweet anise flavor with slightly minty undertones. It can be quite pungent depending on the time of year, so just add a little at a time to see how you like it. No hyssop? Try using one of the thymes, perhaps lemon- or orange-scented thyme.

Heat the olive oil in a large skillet, add the guinea fowl skin side down, and sear the skin until golden. Remove from the pan and carefully cut a pocket in each breast to contain the filling.

To make the filling, put the cheese and hyssop or thyme in a bowl. Add 1 tablespoon of the honey, 2 teaspoons of the orange flower water, salt, and pepper, then mash well. Use to stuff the pockets in the breasts.

Arrange the breasts in the oven dish. Mix the remaining orange flower water with ⅓ cup water and pour over the breasts. Poach in a preheated oven at 400°F for 25 minutes until cooked.

Remove from the oven, put the breasts on a plate, and cover with foil. Keep in a warm place for 8 minutes. Transfer the juices to a small saucepan and reduce over medium heat until reduced by one-third. Stir in the remaining honey to make a syrup.

To serve, cut the breasts diagonally, then serve on warm dinner plates, trickle the syrup over the top, and serve with a pretty herb and flower salad.

- basil
- cilantro

RICH LAMB STEW WITH BASIL AND CILANTRO

¼ cup olive oil

1½ lb. boneless leg of lamb, cut into 1-inch chunks

2 large onions, chopped

2 garlic cloves, crushed

2 sweet red Cubanelle peppers, seeded and chopped

4 ripe tomatoes, peeled, seeded, and coarsely chopped

½ teaspoon cayenne pepper

1 cup fresh vegetable stock or water

10 prunes

10 dried apricots

4 oz. okra, trimmed, about ½ cup

2 Granny Smith apples, peeled, cored, and cubed

1¾ cups canned chickpeas, drained and rinsed

freshly squeezed juice of ½ lemon, or to taste

1 pomegranate, cut in half

a medium bunch of basil

a medium bunch of cilantro

sea salt and freshly ground black pepper

serves 6–8

This is my version of *bozbash*, an Armenian rich lamb stew, packed full with herbs and fruity delicious flavors and textures. Garlic was not used traditionally, but I like it with all these rich flavors. Pomegranates are a typical ingredient in this part of the world—sweet yet tart, with glorious color, but leave them out if they're not in season. Potatoes are usually cooked in the stew, but I prefer a baked potato with lots of butter melting in its open top, giving a contrast in texture. The herbs must be added before serving to keep their aromatic freshness.

Heat a large ovenproof casserole dish over high heat, add 2 tablespoons of the oil, then add the lamb in batches and brown on all sides. Remove to a plate, add 1 tablespoon of oil to the casserole, add the onions, garlic, and red peppers and sauté gently over low heat for 10 minutes.

Increase the heat and add the tomatoes and cayenne and cook until bubbling, about 5 minutes. Add the browned lamb, the stock or water, salt, and pepper and bring to a gentle simmer. Cover with a lid and cook in a preheated oven at 400°F for 20–30 minutes until just softening. Add the prunes and apricots and cook for a further 10 minutes.

Heat the remaining 1 tablespoon of oil in a skillet, add the okra and apple, and sauté for 5 minutes. Transfer the okra, apple, and chickpeas to the casserole and cook for 10 minutes. Test the meat for tenderness. If not yet done, lower the oven to 350°F and cook for a further 10 minutes. Just before serving, squeeze the juice from half the pomegranate and fold into the stew. Coarsely chop the herbs and fold half into the stew. Serve sprinkled with the remaining herbs and the seeds from the remaining pomegranate half.

LEG OF LAMB STUFFED WITH DATES, HERBS, AND SPICES

⅓ cup extra virgin olive oil

2 onions, finely chopped

a large pinch of saffron threads

4 garlic cloves, 2 crushed, 2 sliced

12 lavender or rosemary leaves, chopped, plus extra flower sprigs to serve

¼ teaspoon ground cinnamon

1 teaspoon ground cumin

2 tablespoons pine nuts, toasted

10 Medjool dates, pitted and coarsely chopped

3 lb. leg of lamb (about 2½ lb. after boning)

sea salt and freshly ground black pepper

a roasting pan with a rack

serves 6

You can buy legs of lamb part-boned, with the shank end of the leg left in and the thighbone removed to leave a pocket for the stuffing. If you can't find one, ask the butcher to do it for you, or do it yourself. Ask for it to be tunnel-boned rather than butterflied. Take note of the weight of the meat, so you will know how long to cook it. The stuffing is flavored with the strong aromas of lavender or rosemary. I add extra sprigs to the lamb for the last 5 minutes to flavor the outside. The strength of the herb depends on the time of year—the leaves of spring and early summer will be milder than in high summer, when the volatile oils are at their strongest from the heat of the sun.

To make the stuffing, heat 5 tablespoons of the oil in a skillet, add the onions, saffron, and crushed garlic, and sauté until soft and golden. Add the chopped lavender or rosemary, the cinnamon, cumin, pine nuts, dates, salt, and pepper and mix well. Remove from the heat and let cool. If time allows, prepare it ahead and keep in the refrigerator to mature the flavors.

Push the stuffing into the boned section of the meat. Secure closed with skewers (or sew up with twine). If the meat has been in the refrigerator, let it come back to room temperature. Set on a rack in a roasting pan and add about 1 cup water to the pan. With the point of a knife, cut tiny pockets in the meat, push in the sliced garlic, then season well with salt and pepper.

Cook in a preheated oven at 400°F for 20 minutes, then lower the heat to 350°F and cook for a further 15 minutes for each 1 lb. of lamb. Top up with a few teaspoons of water if it dries out to stop the bits burning on the pan. Five minutes before the end, tuck the flower sprigs into the holes in the meat. Remove from the oven and let it rest on a warm serving dish for 15 minutes before slicing to serve. Check with a meat thermometer if you have one—the internal temperature should be about 135°F.

- cilantro
- bay leaves (left)

PORTUGUESE PORK AND CLAMS WITH BAY LEAVES

2 lb. pork shoulder steaks

1¼ cups extra virgin olive oil

about ¼ teaspoon salt

1 onion, finely chopped

½ cup white wine

1 lb. potatoes, cut into ½-inch cubes

a handful of cilantro leaves, plus extra sprigs to serve

1 lb. small fresh hardshell clams, in the shell

sea salt and freshly ground black pepper

lemon wedges, to serve

marinade

2 tablespoons red sweet pepper cream (crema di pepperoni)*

1 tablespoon sweet paprika

1 chile, seeded and finely chopped

2 whole cloves

2 fresh bay leaves

5 garlic cloves, crushed

serves 4

*available from good delicatessens

Pork and clams—carne de porco a Alentejana—make a simple meal from southern Portugal, a region where bay, cilantro, and garlic richly flavor the dishes. Apart from Portugal and parts of Spain, cilantro isn't a traditional herb in European cooking. Prepare this dish in advance, then steam open the clams and add the herbs at the last minute.

To make the marinade, put the pepper cream, paprika, chile, cloves, bay leaves, and garlic in a glass or ceramic bowl. Cut the pork into chunks and add to the bowl, then add 4 tablespoons of the oil and mix to coat the meat. Let marinate for 2 hours or overnight in the refrigerator.

Thirty minutes before cooking, remove the pork from the refrigerator and sprinkle it with the salt. When ready to cook, heat 1 tablespoon of the oil in a flameproof casserole, add the onion and sauté for 7 minutes until softened but not colored. Remove to a plate. Add 2 tablespoons more oil, then sear the meat in batches on both sides over high heat. As each is browned, transfer to a plate using a slotted spoon. Increase the heat, add the wine, and boil hard for 30 seconds. Add the pork, salt, and pepper, cover with a lid, and cook in a preheated oven at 350°F for 40 minutes. Remove the lid and cook, uncovered, for a further 5 minutes.

Just before serving, heat the remaining oil in a large skillet, add the potatoes, and sauté until tender and golden on all sides. Keep them warm until ready to serve. Chop the cilantro leaves.

Put the clams in a saucepan with about 3 tablespoons water. Cover with a lid, bring to a boil and cook until the clams open, about 3–4 minutes. Discard any that don't open. Remove the clams from the pan and strain the juices through a cheesecloth-lined sieve set over a bowl. Add the juices to the casserole, then stir in the chopped cilantro. Add the opened clams, potatoes and sprigs of cilantro, then serve.

PORK WITH LEMONGRASS, GINGER, AND CHILES

3 lb. piece of boneless pork shoulder

½ teaspoon ground star anise

½ teaspoon ground Szechuan pepper

1 tablespoon safflower oil

8 banana shallots, finely sliced, about 8 oz.

2 inches fresh ginger, peeled and finely sliced

4 garlic cloves, finely sliced

2 stalks of lemongrass, split lengthwise and bruised

1 large red chile, seeded and finely chopped

sea salt

to serve

1 tablespoon safflower oil

a bunch of scallions, sliced diagonally

about 2 cups cooked jasmine rice

6 sprigs of cilantro

a casserole dish, just big enough to hold the pork

serves 4–6

The clean citrus flavor of lemongrass and Chinese spices really permeates the flesh of the pork. Slow cooking is perfect for pork shoulder: it has a high fat content and cooks to a texture that cuts like butter, perfect hot or cold.

Rub the pork with the star anise, Szechuan pepper, and salt. Put the oil, shallots, ginger, garlic, lemongrass, and chile in a casserole dish just big enough to fit the piece of pork. Stir well, then put the pork on top. Cover with a lid and cook in a preheated oven at 350°F for 20 minutes. Lower the oven temperature to 300°F and cook for a further 1 hour 40 minutes.

Slice the pork into bite-size pieces. Heat a wok over medium heat, add the scallions, stir-fry for 30 seconds, then add the pork and the contents of the casserole. Add the cooked jasmine rice and stir-fry until heated through. Add the cilantro and serve.

SAGE AND POTATO GRATIN
WITH BACON AND ONIONS

2 lb. medium boiling potatoes, peeled

1 small onion, halved and finely sliced

1¼ cups heavy cream

14 oz. bacon

12–18 sage leaves

2 tablespoons unsalted butter

sea salt and freshly ground black pepper

*a large deep baking dish,
greased with butter*

serves 4–6

Matahami, the French dish of layered bacon, potato, onions, and herbs, is traditionally made with using thyme and unsmoked bacon, but I prefer it with sage and smoked bacon. It was the first dish I mastered in home economics class and I carried it carried home with pride in a Red-Riding-Hood-style basket with my hand-embroidered cover tied to the handles. Salvia, the generic name for sage, is from the Latin word *salvere*, which means "to be in good health." I grow many varieties, all strong and good for culinary purposes, ranging from the variegated leaf, *Salvia officinalis* 'Tricolor' to the beautiful purple-leafed *Salvia officinalis* 'Purpurascens,' but my favorite is the moleskin leaf of the Greek sage, *Salvia fruticosa*.

Put the peeled potatoes in a saucepan of cold water, bring to a boil, and add salt to the water. Cook for 12 minutes or until you can just pierce them with a skewer (they should be not quite cooked). Heat the butter in a skillet, add the onion, and cook until softened and translucent, about 5 minutes. Drain the potatoes and slice as thinly as possible.

Put the cream in a saucepan, bring to a boil, and simmer for 3 minutes. Arrange one-third of the bacon in the prepared baking dish. Put 4 sage leaves on top. Add a layer of half the potatoes, then another of half the onion. Pour in half the cream. Put half the remaining bacon on top and 4 more sage leaves. Use the remaining potatoes and onion in the same way, pour in the remaining cream, then put the remaining bacon and sage on top.

Dot the sage with butter, then bake in a preheated oven at 400°F for 20 minutes. Cover the dish with foil and bake for a further 30 minutes. Using a skewer, test to see if the potatoes are soft all the way through (if necessary, return to the oven, uncovered, for a further 5–10 minutes, making sure that the bacon and sage don't burn).

- oregano (left)
- purple or opal basil

BASIL AND OREGANO SALSA WITH GRILLED STEAK
chimichurri

6 thick sirloin steaks, about 3 lb. total

sea salt and freshly ground black pepper

oil, for brushing

chimichurri

1 small shallot, chopped

3 garlic cloves, crushed

6 sprigs of oregano

a large bunch of purple basil

1 stalk of fresh green peppercorns, or 1 tablespoon green peppercorns preserved in brine

⅔ cup olive oil

1 tablespoon red wine vinegar

1 red chile, seeded and finely chopped

to serve

watercress

sprigs of purple basil

serves 6

This Argentinian pesto-like salsa is usually made with parsley and is served in individual small bowls alongside thick steaks, grilled rare. I have a big bowl of peppery fresh watercress to serve with it. Purple or "opal" basil has a minty, oil of cloves quality to its flavor. The purple-black leaves become brighter and more intense in color when plunged into hot water—this will also revive a flopped bunch within 10 minutes. Oregano is used extensively in Latin American cuisine.

Using a mortar and pestle, pound the shallot and garlic to a coarse paste.

Pull the leaves off the sprigs of oregano and basil and pound into the paste. Remove the peppercorns from the stalk and pound them into the paste. Start adding the oil a little at a time, then pound in the vinegar and chile, keeping the mixture chunky.

Brush the steaks with oil and season well. Heat a ridged stove-top grill pan and, when it starts to smoke, add the steaks, and cook for about 1½–2 minutes on each side. Remove them and let rest in a warm place for 5 minutes. Slice thickly and serve with the chimichurri, watercress, and extra basil.

Cook's note It is traditional to use a mortar and pestle to make the chimichurri. However, use a blender to save time, pulsing to keep the paste as coarse as possible.

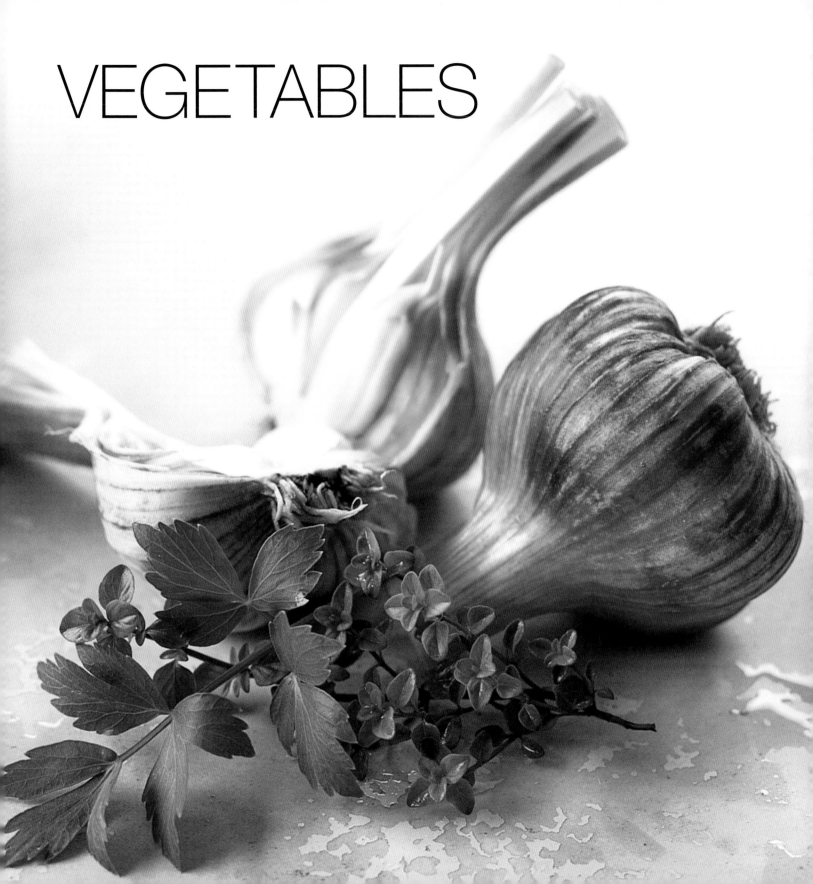

VEGETABLES

● parsley

● marjoram (left)

IMAM BAYILDI

Over the years, I have eaten many versions of this Middle Eastern eggplant dish. Some have been meltingly delicious, others not so nice. The dish got its name because the priest (the Imam) found it so delicious that he swooned. Some stories tell that he really fainted because he was horrified at the amount of oil used to cook it. This is the secret of course—eggplant must be cooked well, with large quantities of oil. So this, for my palate, is the definitive recipe for an ancient dish. It uses the heavily scented marjoram—when it has its knotted flowers in bloom, use those too, plus lots of parsley.

4 large eggplant, with long stalks if possible, halved lengthwise

¾ cup extra virgin olive oil

1 lb. onions, halved and very finely sliced

4 garlic cloves, crushed

1½ lb. Italian plum tomatoes, peeled, seeded, and finely chopped

leaves from 15 sprigs of flat-leaf parsley

leaves from 12 sprigs of marjoram

2 teaspoons sugar

1 small lemon, finely sliced

sea salt and freshly ground black pepper

an ovenproof dish, big enough to hold the eggplant in a single layer

serves 4–8

Cut a line ¼ inch in from the edges of the eggplant halves, then score the flesh inside with a criss-cross pattern. Rub plenty of oil all over the eggplant and season with a little salt. Arrange in a single layer in the ovenproof dish. Cook in a preheated oven at 400°F for about 30 minutes or until the flesh has just softened.

Heat ⅓ cup of the oil in a heavy skillet, add the onions and garlic, cover with a lid, and cook over low heat until soft. Increase the heat and add the tomatoes. Cook until the juices from the tomatoes have reduced a little, then add salt and pepper to taste. Reserve a few parsley leaves for serving, then chop the remainder together with the marjoram. Add to the onion and tomato mixture, then add the sugar.

Scoop some of the central flesh out of the eggplant, leaving a shell around the outside to hold the base in shape. Chop the scooped out section and add to the mixture. Pile the mixture into the eggplant shells and sprinkle with pepper. Arrange the lemon slices on top. Trail more oil generously over the top, then sprinkle with ¼ cup water.

Cover with aluminum foil and bake for 30–40 minutes until meltingly soft. Remove the foil about 10 minutes before the end. Serve, sprinkled with the remaining oil and extra parsley.

SAGE BUTTERED BABY LEEKS
WITH CHILE BREAD CRUMBS

6 tablespoons salted butter

2 tablespoons finely chopped sage

1 lb. short thin young leeks, split halfway through and well washed

2 tablespoons extra virgin olive oil

1 cup fresh ciabatta bread crumbs

1 mild red chile, seeded and finely chopped

1 smaller red chile, seeded and sliced into rings

serves 4

Sage makes a great partnership with leeks, and the Italian-style chile bread crumb dressing makes a delicious combination. For an even more pronounced Italian accent, the crisp crumbs are made from ciabatta bread. If possible, use the mild, tender leaves of the gold variegated sage, *Salvia officinalis* 'Icterina,' for a less "thuggish" medicinal flavor.

Put the butter and sage in a bowl and mash well.

Steam or boil the leeks for about 5 minutes or until tender. Toss in half the sage butter and keep hot.

Heat a skillet, add the oil and ciabatta crumbs, sauté for about 45 seconds, then add the remaining sage butter and all the chiles. Sauté until golden.

Put the leeks on a serving plate, and top with the chile bread crumbs and the sliced smaller chile. Serve with other dishes or as an appetizer.

- lovage (left)
- thyme

ARTICHOKES PROVENÇAL

1 lemon, halved

18–24 baby artichokes, depending on size

3 tablespoons extra virgin olive oil

6 slices bacon, cut into strips crosswise

10 oz. small shallots

3 garlic cloves, halved

4 carrots, halved lengthwise and cut into fine strips

¾ cup white wine

½ cup vegetable stock

2 young sprigs of lovage, or a few celery leaves

a large sprig of thyme

1 cup cooked or canned white beans, such as cannellini

sea salt and freshly ground black pepper

to serve

crusty bread

boiled rice, preferably red Camargue

salad leaves

a heavy shallow ovenproof casserole dish

serves 6

Based on a Provençal dish, baby artichokes are picked before the hairy choke has formed. I use lovage, thyme, and beans in this recipe, cooked in a shallow terracotta dish. Lovage grows well—its strong green leaves push up through the soil in April and will grow as tall as my garden fence if left unused, so I keep it trimmed to ensure a good supply of new leaves. Only a small amount of lovage is needed to give maximum flavor. If you've never tasted it, prepare to be smitten—it's a delightful herb, full of character, similar to celery in some ways.

Squeeze the cut lemon halves into a bowl of cold water and add the lemon skins. Set aside to add the artichokes as they are prepared (the acidulated water will prevent them from discoloring).

To prepare the artichokes, remove about 3 layers of tough leaves from the outside, cut off the top ½ inch of leaves, and trim the stalks to about 1 inch. Using a vegetable peeler, peel the stalks. As you work, add the artichokes to the bowl of lemon water.

Heat 1 tablespoon of oil in the casserole dish, add the bacon, and sauté until crisp and golden. Transfer to a plate.

Add the remaining oil, then sauté the whole shallots and garlic until golden. Drain the artichokes and add them to the pan. Add the carrots and stir-fry for 2 minutes. Add the wine, bring to a boil, and reduce for 2 minutes, Add the stock and simmer for 2 minutes. Add salt, pepper, lovage, and thyme. Cover and cook in a preheated oven at 400°F for 20 minutes until the artichokes are tender. Add the beans and heat through, uncovered, for 5 minutes. Serve with bread, boiled rice, and salad.

• rosemary
• bay leaves (left)

OVEN-ROASTED VEGETABLES,
WITH ROSEMARY, BAY LEAVES, AND GARLIC

1 lb. boiling potatoes,
cut into 2-inch chunks

about 1 lb. butternut squash,
cut into wedges and seeded

6 small red onions, quartered

¼ cup extra virgin olive oil

8 garlic cloves, unpeeled

2 red Cubanelle (long) peppers or bell
peppers, seeded and cut into chunks

4 sprigs of rosemary

4 sprigs of bay leaves

sea salt

a large baking pan

serves 4

Roasted vegetables are made extra special with the strong flavors of herbs. Thyme is good, but I love rosemary (be sparing though—too much can overwhelm a dish). Bay leaves are quite mild when young, so don't use as many if you have mature leaves.

Bring a large saucepan of water to a boil, add salt and the potatoes, and cook for 5 minutes. Drain, then put in a large baking pan. Add the squash, onions, and 2 tablespoons of the oil. Toss to coat, then roast in a preheated oven at 400°F for 10 minutes.

Add 1 extra tablespoon of oil to the baking pan, followed by the garlic and peppers, 2 sprigs of rosemary, and 2 sprigs of bay leaves. Roast at the same temperature for 15 minutes, then add the rest of the herbs and continue roasting for 10–15 minutes. Turn the vegetables occasionally until all are tender and the edges slightly charred. Trail the remaining oil over the top, then serve.

Cook's extra Sprinkle with 3 tablespoons pine nuts and some crumbled feta cheese 5 minutes before the end of the cooking time, so the nuts roast a little and the feta softens.

PASTA, RICE, AND BREAD

- chervil
- flat-leaf parsley
- sweet cicely

HOMEMADE HERB PASTA
WITH HERB OIL

1¼ cups Italian-style pasta flour
or all-purpose flour*

2 large eggs (orange yolks will give a
stronger pasta color)

about 36 fresh herb leaves, such as chervil,
flat-leaf parsley, sweet cicely, or flowers such
as marigolds and nasturtiums (make sure
they aren't damp), plus extra to serve

a small bag of baby spinach, about 8 oz.

3 mild dried chiles, seeded and
ground with a pinch of salt

salt

homemade herb oil, such as basil
or parsley, to serve (page 138)

a pasta machine

serves 4

*Pasta dough made with Italian-style pasta
flour can be made 1 day ahead and
kept refrigerated. Regular all-purpose flour
dough turns grey after 3 hours if
left uncooked.

Homemade herb pasta is fun to make with your children—it's almost like paper making. There is no limit to the fun they can have dashing out to the garden to see if this leaf or that petal will suit. I found this a good way to teach my children what they can eat from the garden.

Put the flour and salt in a food processor and pulse to mix. Put the eggs in a bowl and beat with a fork, then add to the food processor. Pulse until the mixture forms fine balls (like couscous), then transfer to a work surface. Knead to form a ball, then wrap in plastic wrap and chill for 1 hour.

Cut the dough into 3 pieces and wrap each one in plastic wrap. Set the pasta machine to the widest setting. Working with one piece of dough at a time, roll out once, then fold it into 3 layers. Repeat 4 times, no matter how crumbly, in order to achieve a pliable dough.

Gradually narrow the settings, rolling twice through each setting, then put it through the narrowest setting 3 times. Cover the sheet of dough with plastic wrap, then fold into 3, so it is interleaved with plastic. Make sure it is well sealed with plastic to stop it drying out. When all the dough has been rolled out, cut one sheet into 3-inch wide strips and cover with plastic wrap.

Take one strip of pasta and put a herb leaf at one end. Fold over the other end to cover the leaf evenly. Roll twice through the machine on the second narrowest setting to stretch the leaf trapped inside the pasta sandwich. Trim any rough sides, but any odd shapes are fine. Repeat with the remaining dough.

Bring a large saucepan of water to a boil, add 2 teaspoons salt, and cook the pasta in 2 batches for 1 minute each. Add half the spinach with each batch, just before draining, and drain immediately so the spinach is just wilted. Put in warm pasta bowls and sprinkle with the chile salt mixture, and a few marigold petals if using. Trail the green herb oil over the top and serve immediately.

● purple or opal basil (left)

PURPLE BASIL RAVIOLI
WITH TRUFFLE BUTTER

Purple basil, which adds a hint of minty spice to the potato stuffing, is also known as opal basil. The one with a ruffled leaf has an interesting licorice flavor, but is less easy to find unless you grow it yourself. This dish is worth the effort for a special dinner and can be made the day before.

a large pinch of saffron threads

2 large eggs

1⅓ cups Italian-style pasta flour
or all-purpose flour

1 lb. purple-or-blue fleshed potatoes

⅔ cup finely grated Manchego cheese

a large handful of purple basil sprigs

1 egg white

sea salt

truffle oil, to serve

truffle butter

2 oz. jar black truffles

5–6 tablespoons unsalted butter,
cut into pieces

a pasta machine

2-inch fluted ravioli cutter

serves 4–6, makes 36 ravioli

*Note I prefer to freeze the ravioli
and cook from frozen, which stops them
sticking together.*

To make the pasta dough, use a mortar and pestle to grind the saffron to a fine powder with a little salt. Add the eggs one at a time and mix thoroughly. Put the flour in a food processor and pulse for a second, then add the egg mixture. Pulse until the mixture forms fine balls (like couscous), then transfer to a work surface. Knead to form a ball, then wrap in plastic, and chill for 1 hour.

Meanwhile, put the potatoes in a saucepan, add a pinch of salt, and cover with cold water. Bring to a boil, add salt, and cook until the potatoes are very soft. Drain and, when cool enough to handle, peel off the skins. Mash and let cool, then stir in the Manchego. Remove the leaves from the basil, chop, and add to the potato mixture.

Cut the pasta dough into 3 pieces and wrap each one in plastic. Set the pasta machine to the widest setting. Working with one piece of dough at a time, roll out once, then fold it into 3 layers. Repeat 4 times, no matter how crumbly, in order to achieve a pliable dough.

Gradually narrow the settings, rolling twice through each setting, then put it through the narrowest setting 3 times until you have a long thin sheet. Cover the sheet of dough with plastic wrap, then fold into 3, so it is interleaved with plastic. Make sure it is well sealed with plastic to stop it drying out. When all the dough has been rolled out, cut each sheet into 12 strips, 3 inches wide. Cover with plastic wrap.

Put 1 teaspoon of potato mixture on one end and brush some egg white around it. Fold the dough strip over and seal it, expelling any air as you work. Stamp out around the filling using the ravioli cutter. Use a little extra flour if the dough is too soft.

To make the truffle butter, slice one large truffle thinly and chop the rest. Put the chopped truffle in a blender and add the butter.

To cook the pasta, bring a large saucepan of lightly salted water to a boil. Add the pasta and cook for 2–3 minutes. Drain, reserving ⅔ cup cooking water and blend it with the butter and chopped truffles. Pour the truffle butter over the pasta, toss gently, then serve topped with the sliced truffle and a few drops of truffle oil.

- flat-leaf parsley
- borage
- lemon geranium

FRESH HERB RISOTTO

3⅓ cups light vegetable stock

1 stick unsalted butter

2 tablespoons extra virgin olive oil

2 red onions, finely chopped

1½ cups Italian risotto rice, such as arborio

½ cup white wine

a handful of borage leaves

2 yellow squash, about 12 oz., cut into ½-inch cubes

8 oz. thin or wild asparagus

a handful of flat-leaf parsley leaves

a few lemon geranium leaves (optional)

1 cup arugula

sea salt and freshly ground black pepper

to serve (optional)

1¼ cups fresh Parmesan cheese shavings

a few borage flowers

serves 4–6

I love this risotto for its summer quality—using up all those yellow squash. Lemon geranium leaves are added for their citrus tang, plus borage leaves, which give a cucumber flavor. I use it instead of spinach and prefer the young leaves—I make use of the flowers too to scatter over the dish. Take care when picking borage—the leaves are a bit furry and can produce a rash. Use gloves if you're sensitive. The only one to eat (leaves and flowers) is *Borago officinalis*. It gave Roman soldiers courage, although I can't imagine a tough legionary chewing on a blue, star-shaped flower.

Put the stock in a saucepan, bring to a boil, then keep over very low heat.

Put half the butter and all the oil in a heavy skillet and heat until the butter melts. Add the onions and cook until softened and translucent.

Stir in the rice and turn to coat in the hot oil. Increase the heat and add the wine, which will splutter and eventually be absorbed. Add half the borage leaves, then stir in 1 ladle of hot stock.

Add the squash and asparagus. Coarsely chop the parsley leaves. Add 1 tablespoon of the parsley and the lemon geranium leaves, if using, then another ladle of stock. Keep adding the stock as it is absorbed.

When the rice is cooked, but still *al dente*, add the remaining borage leaves and butter, arugula, parsley, and salt and pepper to taste. Remove and discard the lemon geranium leaves.

Serve, topped with Parmesan shavings and a few borage flowers, if using.

Cook's note Because borage and lemon geraniums are only available to people who grow them in their own gardens, they can be replaced with 1½ inches cucumber (instead of borage) and the finely peeled zest of 1 lemon (instead of lemon geranium). Remove both before serving.

- curry leaves (left)
- cilantro

RICE AND LENTILS WITH HERBS
bhooni kitcheri

2¼ cups whole red lentils (masoor dhaal)

2¼ cups basmati rice

6 tablespoons unsalted butter

12 curry leaves or 3 bay leaves

1 inch fresh ginger, peeled and grated

2 garlic cloves, crushed

½ teaspoon hot red pepper flakes

peanut or safflower oil, for frying

10 shallots, banana or regular, about 14 oz., finely sliced

a large bunch of cilantro, coarsely chopped

3 fresh green chiles, seeded and finely chopped

sea salt and freshly ground black pepper

to serve

4 hard-cooked eggs, quartered

2 lemons, cut into wedges

a heat diffuser

serves 6

The Indian *kitcheri*, meaning "a bit of a mess" or a porridge, was the precursor to the British colonial dish of kedgeree. The *bhooni* part of the title means the porridge is dry, not wet. Fragrant curry leaves are sold in big bunches in Indian greengrocers, but if unavailable, use bay leaves or a kaffir lime leaf instead. This is a wonderful dish, and if you want to give it a flavor of the Raj, add a poached smoked haddock and eggs at the last minute. Any whole lentils can be used, but beware of Puy lentils, which will turn the rice a rather unattractive grey color. I find whole red lentils from Indian stores taste best, but whole Italian brown lentils are excellent, too. There is a large quantity of cilantro in this dish, but it's very good—don't skimp.

Put the lentils in a bowl, cover with cold water, and let soak for 30 minutes. Put the rice in a strainer and wash under cold running water until the water runs clear. Drain the lentils and rice.

Put the butter in a large saucepan and heat until melted. Add the drained lentils and rice and stir to coat with butter. Add 4 of the curry leaves or all the bay leaves, the ginger, garlic, hot red pepper flakes, salt, and pepper. Cover with 3¾ cups cold water, stir, and bring to a boil. As soon as it boils, cover with a lid and lower the heat to low (use a heat diffuser). Cook for 30 minutes.

Meanwhile, heat the oil in a skillet, add the remaining curry leaves, and sauté for 10 seconds. Remove and drain on paper towels—the leaves become crisp as they cool. Add the shallots in 2 batches and sauté until crisp and golden. As they are ready, remove and drain on paper towels.

When the kitcheri is ready, fluff it up with a fork and fold in the cilantro and two-thirds of the fried shallots and all the chopped chiles. To serve, fluff up with a fork and top with the fried curry leaves, the remaining fried shallots, hard-cooked eggs and lemon wedges.

SAGE SCHIACCIATA BREAD
WITH CHEESE AND ONION

2⅓ cups unbleached bread flour

½ teaspoon salt

1 envelope or 1 tablespoon fast-acting dried yeast

2 tablespoons olive oil, plus extra to serve

4 large sage leaves, coarsely chopped

cheese and onion topping

3 tablespoons olive oil

½ cup grated Manchego cheese

1 red onion or 4 pink Thai shallots, sliced into rings

8 sage leaves, chopped

sea salt flakes and freshly ground black pepper

a baking tray, dusted with flour

serves 6–8

The Italian word *schiacciata* means "flattened," which is how this focaccia-style bread gets its name. This version is flavored with sage, which has always been seen as a healthy herb, famous for its antiseptic qualities. It can have a very strong, medicinal flavor, so it should be used sparingly.

Put the flour, salt, and yeast in a large bowl and mix well. Put the oil in measuring cup, add 1 cup hot water, and stir well. Make a hollow in the flour and pour in the liquid. Mix with your hand and, when it all comes together, transfer to a floured work surface. Knead for 5 minutes until the dough is elastic. Put the dough in an oiled bowl, cover, and let rise in a warm place for 1 hour.

Transfer the dough to a work surface, add the sage, and knead for 2–3 minutes. Put the dough on a baking sheet and shape it into a flat circle about 9 inches diameter, then make indentations all over the surface of the dough with your fingers. Brush with the 3 tablespoons of olive oil and leave at room temperature for 10 minutes.

Cook in a preheated oven at 400°F for 10 minutes. Remove from the oven, spread the grated cheese on top, followed by the onion rings, freshly ground black pepper, and chopped sage leaves. Cook for a further 10 minutes, then increase the heat to 425°F and cook for another 5 minutes or until done. To test, insert a skewer in the middle. It should come out clean—if it doesn't, cook for 5 minutes longer.

Sprinkle with sea salt flakes and more olive oil, then serve.

PISSALADIERE

Pissaladière is the Provençal version of pizza. I like to cook the onion topping in white wine and extra virgin olive oil—the tastes are intense, so they need a challenging sister flavor, such as the highly aromatic, pine-like qualities of rosemary. Though it isn't traditional, I like to add roasted red bell pepper for a hint of color.

1¾ cups all-purpose flour

2 teaspoons fast-acting dried yeast

½ teaspoon salt

1 egg, beaten

1 tablespoon extra virgin olive oil

topping

2 lb. white onions, thinly sliced

2 tablespoons brown sugar

½ cup extra virgin olive oil

⅔ cup white wine

1 sprig of rosemary and 2 tablespoons chopped rosemary leaves

1 large red Cubanelle (long) pepper or bell pepper

2 teaspoons anchovy paste

4 oz. canned anchovies, drained and halved lengthwise

about 20 black olives

freshly ground black pepper

a baking sheet with sides, about 12 x 10 inches

serves 6–8

To make the dough, put the flour, yeast, and salt in a large bowl and mix briefly. Put the egg and oil in a small bowl, add ⅔ cup hot water, and beat well. Make a hollow in the flour and pour in the egg mixture. Using your hand, mix until the dough comes together into a ball. Transfer to a floured work surface and knead for about 5 minutes until soft and elastic. Transfer the dough to an oiled bowl, cover with plastic wrap, and let rise in a warm place for 1 hour.

To make the topping, put the onions in a large saucepan. Stir in the sugar, ¼ cup of the oil, the wine, and a sprig of rosemary. Cook over low heat for 30 minutes, turning every 10 minutes so the onions don't burn. The liquid should evaporate, leaving the onions soft and deliciously perfumed.

Using a toasting fork or tongs, hold the red pepper over a gas flame and char until blackened all over. Put into a plastic bag and let steam for 10 minutes to soften. Rub off the skin under the faucet, then remove the seeds and slice the flesh into thin lengths. Set aside.

Transfer the dough to a floured work surface and knead for 1 minute. Roll out to a rough rectangle, then put into the baking tray, pushing the dough to the edges and fitting it into the corners. Mix the anchovy paste with 2 tablespoons of the oil and smooth onto the dough base. Brush the edges with more oil. Remove the sprig of rosemary from the onions and stir in the chopped rosemary. Pour the mixture over the dough. Arrange the anchovies and pepper strips side by side in a diamond pattern and leave for 10 minutes at room temperature. Bake in a preheated oven at 375°F for about 20 minutes. Remove from the oven, put the olives in the center of each diamond, pour over the remaining oil, sprinkle with pepper, and return to the oven for a further 5 minutes (cover with foil if over-browning). Serve warm or at room temperature.

SWEET THINGS

SUMMER FRUIT SALAD
WITH KAFFIR LIME SORBET

a handful of kaffir lime leaves

1¼ cups sugar

⅔ cup white wine

1 egg white

1 cantaloupe melon, halved and seeded

1 honeydew melon, halved and seeded

1 small watermelon,
preferably seedless, halved

2 ripe mangoes, cheeks removed

4 large kiwifruit, peeled

1 dragon fruit, peeled (optional)

*an ice cream maker
or freezer-proof container*

melon ballers

serves 4–6

**Dragon fruit is a large pink tropical fruit
covered with green and yellow horns. Its
flesh is sweet, with tiny black seeds like
vanilla. It is sold in Chinese and Asian
markets, and sometimes in upscale
produce stores and supermarkets.
If unavailable, omit or use another tropical
fruit, such as papaya.*

Use any fruit that you can scoop out with a melon baller for this salad. The kaffir lime leaf, with its clean citrus flavors, is used to perfume the syrup. Pour the syrup over the fruit and churn the remainder into a soft sorbet. It seems like a lot of leaves but it works. Buy them in big bags from Chinese or Asian markets, then use them fresh or freeze and use straight from frozen. Any leftovers may be used to make Thai curries. They grow in pairs, as shown.

Tear the lime leaves and arrange in layers in a saucepan, sprinkling the sugar between the layers. Set aside for several hours or overnight to develop the flavors. Add 1 cup water and slowly heat to dissolve the sugar. Boil for 1 minute and transfer to a bowl to chill.

Strain the syrup and measure ¾ cup into a bowl. Add the wine and ½ cup water and chill in the refrigerator. Set the remainder aside until you are ready to make the salad.

Add the egg white to the syrup and wine and beat just to break it up. Transfer to an ice cream maker and churn according to the manufacturer's instructions. Eat immediately or store in the freezer. Alternatively, put the mixture into a large freezer-proof container and freeze, stirring occasionally to break up the ice crystals.

When ready to serve, scoop balls of fruit into a bowl using one or several sizes of melon ballers. Pour the reserved syrup over the top and keep cool until needed. Serve with scoops of sorbet.

LEMONGRASS-GINGER SYRUP
WITH DRAGON'S EYES

1¼ cups sugar

1 inch fresh ginger, peeled and thinly sliced

3 stalks of lemongrass, bruised and coarsely chopped

2 star fruit (carambola)

36 fresh longans or lychees, peeled and seeded, or 2 cans, about 16 oz. each, drained

finely grated zest and juice of 1 lime

2 baking sheets, lined with silicone baking parchment

serves 6

"Dragon's eyes" is the romantic name for the longan fruit, a relative of the lychee, which you can use instead, either fresh or canned, though I prefer canned. Longans, which look like huge bunches of brown hairy grapes, are only available fresh in fall, and you'll see special vendors selling them in Asian markets. Lemongrass and ginger are the distinctive flavors of Thailand. They make an easy syrup for this simple dessert to finish a Thai-style dinner and, like other Asian ingredients, are easy to use from frozen.

Put the sugar and 1½ cups water in a heavy saucepan and heat gently to dissolve. Increase the heat, add the ginger and lemongrass, and boil for 8 minutes until syrupy but still pale. Remove from the heat and let cool completely.

To make the star fruit crisps, peel off the brown ridges of the starfruit with a vegetable peeler. Slice the fruit crosswise very thinly using a mandoline. Arrange them on paper towels. Brush the top side with a little of the cold syrup and set them on the prepared baking sheets, painted side down. Lightly brush the top side with syrup. Transfer to a preheated oven and cook at 225°F. Gently turn them over after 30 minutes, return to the oven, and dry them out for a further 15 minutes. Carefully peel off the paper.

Strain the syrup, leaving in a few bits of ginger. Add the longans, lime juice, and zest to the cold syrup and chill until ready to serve with the crisps.

Cook's extra To test if the star fruit crisps are ready, take one out, it should crisp as it cools. They can be kept stored in an airtight container until ready to use.

- **tansy leaves**
- **viola flowers**

TANSY PANNA COTTA

a medium bunch of fresh young tansy
leaves, sweet cicely, or 6 bay leaves

2½ cups heavy cream

3 tablespoons sugar

2½ oz. white chocolate drops

1 sachet powdered gelatine

candied flowers (optional)

1 egg white

a large handful of violas or violets

sugar (see method)

6 ramekins or other small molds, ½ cup each

a heat diffuser

serves 6

Tansy is an old-fashioned herb, which is available at many garden
centers, and is very useful in the garden as a pest controller. A
perennial, it grows to a fine height. It has bright yellow, button-like
flowers and was used in Victorian nosegays. If unavailable, use sweet
cicely or flavor the cream with six bay leaves.

To candy the flowers, put the egg white in a bowl and beat lightly to break it up.
Paint the flowers lightly with the egg white, then put the sugar in a tea strainer
and sprinkle it over the top. Transfer to parchment paper and leave in a warm,
dry place until crisp. Store in an airtight container for up to 1 week.

To prepare the panna cotta, strip the fern-like young tansy leaves from the
center stem or the sweet cicely leaves in the same way. Purée in a blender with
¼ cup water and ¼ cup of the cream. Pour through a nylon sieve set over a
bowl and press out the juice with a ladle and reserve (discard the pulp).

Put the remaining cream in a saucepan and heat gently over low heat to just
below boiling point (use a heat diffuser so it takes about 15 minutes). Add the
sugar and chocolate and mix to dissolve. Soften the gelatin in cold water for
10 minutes, add to the pan, and stir to dissolve. Cool for 20 minutes. Add the
tansy or sweet cicely juice and stir well.

Arrange the ramekins on a tray, pour in the mixture, cover, and chill to set. To
serve, unmold the panna cottas by dipping the bases in hot water and inverting
onto plates. Top with the candied flowers.

ROSE MERINGUETTES
WITH ROSE GERANIUM SYRUP

12 rose-scented geranium leaves

¾ cup sugar

1 teaspoon red sugar crystals
(from the baking section of the supermarket
or speciality suppliers)

2 extra large egg whites

a pinch of cream of tartar

candied leaves and petals*

petals from 4 small rosebuds

a handful of rose geranium flowers

small leaves from the top of
rose geranium sprigs

1 egg white

sugar (see method)

chantilly cream

1¼ cups heavy cream

2 teaspoons sifted confectioners' sugar

1 teaspoon rosewater

2 baking sheets, lined with baking parchment

makes 12

**Ensure the leaves and petals have not been
sprayed with anything harmful.*

These meringues have rose-scented sugar as their base. Scented geraniums are available at garden centers—ask for *Pelargonium capitatum* (rose-scented geranium) or just the variety Attar of Roses. It is the leaves, rather than the flowers, that have the strongest scent. Native to South Africa, these plants have been popular since the 17th century. For the best scent, let the sugar sit with the leaves for 4 days. Alternatively, just use a few extra drops of rosewater in the mixture or strongly scented unsprayed rose petals.

To candy the leaves and petals, follow the method on the previous page.

To scent the sugar, put the geranium leaves and sugar in an airtight jar and set aside for 4 days. When ready to make the meringues, remove the scented leaves from the sugar and discard the leaves. Put 5 tablespoons of the sugar into a clean electric coffee grinder, add the red sugar crystals, and grind to a fine powder.

Put the egg whites and cream of tartar in a bowl and beat until firm peaks form. Beat in the remaining ½ cup scented sugar, a spoonful at a time. Gently fold in the pink sugar powder a little at a time.

Spoon 12 piles onto the baking sheets and cook in a preheated oven at 225°F for about 1 hour (open the oven door a little if bubbles appear). Remove from the oven after 1 hour or until firm. Leave for 5 minutes in the cool air and peel off the paper. Put them back on the paper to cool completely. Store in an airtight container until needed.

To make the chantilly cream, put the cream, confectioners' sugar, and rosewater in a bowl and beat until soft peaks form. Use the cream to sandwich the meringues together, then serve sprinkled with candied leaves and petals.

FIG ON A CUSHION WITH THYME-SCENTED SYRUP

1 lb. puff pastry dough, fresh or frozen

6 sprigs of thyme, with flowers if available

⅓ cup sugar

2 teaspoons grenadine (pomegranate syrup)

6–7 oz. triple-crème cheese, such as Saint André, cut horizontally to make 4 disks

6 fresh ripe figs, preferably purple, halved vertically

1 egg yolk, beaten with 2 teaspoons water

2 dough cutters or templates, about 6 and 4 inches diameter

serves 4

Dessert and cheese in one, this tart was inspired by chef Paul Gayler from London's Lanesborough Hotel. He uses shortcrust pastry dough, blue cheese, and pears in his version. I use my favorite broad-leaved thyme, the creeping *Thymus pulegiuides*. It's in leaf all year round with mauve flowers in summer. Orange-scented thyme—*Thymus fragrantissimus*—would provide another interesting flavor.

Let the dough thaw if frozen, then put it on a floured surface and roll out to about 12 inches square. Using the 6-inch dough cutter or template, cut out 4 circles. Use the edge of the knife to separate the layers of dough so they will rise well. Set the circles on the baking sheet and chill for 30 minutes.

Strip the leaves off 4 sprigs of thyme and put them in a small saucepan. Add the sugar and ⅓ cup water. Set over medium heat and slowly dissolve the sugar. Boil for 4 minutes. Remove from the heat, add the grenadine, let cool, then chill.

Make slashes at ½-inch intervals around the edges of the dough circles and score an inner circle to join up the slashes—don't cut all the way through. Prick the inside of each circle with a fork.

Put 1 round of cheese in the middle of each piece of dough. Strip the leaves off the remaining 2 sprigs of thyme and sprinkle on top of the cheese. Arrange 3 fig halves on each piece of cheese.

Brush around the edges of the dough with the beaten egg yolk, but don't let it drip down the sides or they won't rise. Chill until ready to cook. Bake in a preheated oven at 425°F for 20–25 minutes until puffed and golden. Strain the scented syrup, pour it over the figs, add a few pink thyme flowers, if using, then serve.

LAVENDER AND TANGERINE ALMOND CAKES

3 mandarins or other small oranges, such as clementines or tangerines

1 stick unsalted butter, cut into small pieces

2½ cups slivered almonds, ground in a food processor to a fine meal

4 large eggs, separated

lavender flowers, on stems, to decorate

lavender sugar

1¼ cups sugar

3 sprigs of flowering lavender

lavender frosting

1 teaspoon lavender petals

¼ cup sugar

1 cup confectioners' sugar

lavender food coloring (optional)

6 ramekins or dariole molds, ⅔ cup each

parchment paper

serves 6

I am a lavender devotee. There was a time when it was seen as the special province of old ladies. Well not any more—it is enjoying a much-deserved renaissance. Its calming and relaxing qualities soothe away pain and encourage tranquil sleep. In the kitchen, its flavor is superb and its color delightful.

To make the lavender sugar, put the sugar in an airtight container, add the sprigs of lavender, and leave overnight. Remove the sprigs before using.

Cut pieces of parchment paper 2 inches higher than the molds, then use to line them.

Put the whole mandarins in a saucepan, cover with water, and simmer for about 30 minutes, taking care not to let them split. Carefully remove and discard the stalks. Drain the mandarins and put them in a blender. Add the butter, almonds, and half the lavender sugar and blend until smooth.

Put the remaining sugar in a bowl, add the egg yolks, and beat until pale and thick. Gently fold in the orange mixture.

Put the egg whites in a bowl and beat until soft peaks form. Fold gently into the orange mixture, then use to fill the lined molds, ½ cm higher than the top of the mold.

Transfer to a preheated oven and bake at 375°F for about 40 minutes. Pierce with a skewer—if it comes out clean, they are done. Remove from the oven, let cool for 10 minutes, then invert onto a wire rack to cool completely. If overbrowning, cover and reduce the heat to 350°F until done.

To make the frosting, put the lavender petals and sugar in a coffee grinder and work to a fine powder. Sift it and the confectioners' sugar into a bowl, then stir in about 2 tablespoons water to make a smooth but not too runny frosting. If it is too pale, add a tiny drop of food coloring. Turn the cakes the right way up and spoon the frosting over the cakes. Top with lavender sprigs or petals and serve. Eat within 2 days.

MOROCCAN MELISSA PASTRIES

1¼ cups shelled pistachios

1½ cups slivered almonds, ground to a find meal in a food processor

½ cup confectioners' sugar

⅓ cup sugar

½ teaspoon ground cinnamon, plus extra to serve

2 teaspoons rose water or orange flower water

a handful of lemon balm (melissa) or lemon verbena, finely chopped

1½ sticks unsalted butter

8 large sheets of phyllo pastry dough

2 tablespoons confectioners' sugar, sifted

a baking sheet

makes 8

This crumbly Moroccan pastry is usually flavored with mint and finely grated lemon zest. In place of lemon and mint (which you can use instead), I use a close relation of mint—lemon balm—or fragrant lemon verbena, which is in leaf most of the year in my garden. Lemon balm is also known by its pretty name, melissa, from the Greek word for honey bee. It grows like a weed in my garden and I never want to stop it or tame it because it smells so marvelous. It also makes a cool, invigorating drink at the height of summer.

Put the pistachios in a clean coffee grinder and grind to a fine powder. Reserve 2 tablespoons of the pistachio powder to decorate the finished pastries. Put the remainder in a bowl, add the ground almonds, confectioners' sugar, sugar, cinnamon, rosewater, and lemon balm or lemon verbena.

Soften 1 stick of the butter to room temperature and mash into the nut mixture to form a paste. Chill for 10 minutes, then divide into 8 portions.

Melt the remaining butter in a small saucepan. Arrange 1 sheet of phyllo on a work surface with the long edge towards you (keep the rest covered so it doesn't dry out). Brush the edges of the sheet with melted butter and spread one portion of the paste in a line on the front edge of the phyllo—leave it loose with a few gaps, so it doesn't split when turned in a spiral. Roll it up, away from you to make a thin log, then brush with a little more butter to make it pliable. Coil the log into a spiral and tuck the end underneath to seal. Brush with extra butter and put on a baking sheet. Repeat to make 8 spirals in all.

Bake in a preheated oven at 400°F for 20–25 minutes until golden.

Remove from the oven and let cool on a wire rack. Dust with confectioners' sugar, then sprinkle the reserved ground pistachio powder and cinnamon over the top in wriggly lines.

LITTLE EXTRAS

HERB BUTTERS

Herb or "compound" butters, as they are known, are handy to have in the refrigerator or freezer—just add a spoonful to fish, grilled meat, hot potatoes, or other vegetables. The flavors trapped in the butter are a revelation, so experiment with different herbs. Here are some ideas to start you off!

CHIVRY BUTTER

a large bunch of mixed herbs such as parsley, tarragon, chervil, salad burnett, and chives

1½ sticks salted butter

1½ tablespoons finely chopped shallot

makes 1 cup

Strip the leaves off the stalks and blanch in a saucepan of boiling water for 30 seconds. Tip into a colander and refresh under cold running water.

Drain, pat dry, and chop coarsely. Melt 2 tablespoons of the butter in a small skillet, add the shallot, and cook over low heat until slightly softened but not browned, about 2 minutes. Let cool.

Pour into a food processor, then add the herbs and remaining butter. Pulse until smooth, then transfer to a sheet of wax paper or plastic wrap and roll into a log. Alternatively, spoon into little butter dishes, smooth off the tops with a knife, then chill until firm.

NASTURTIUM AND SAVORY BUTTER

1½ sticks salted butter

5 sprigs of savory

8 nasturtium leaves

8 nasturtium flowers

makes ¾ cup

Strip the leaves from the savory and chop them finely. Chop the nasturtium leaves and flowers. Put in a food processor and pulse to mix.

BASIL, PINE NUT, AND CHILE BUTTER

50 g pine nuts, lightly toasted in a dry skillet

4 tablespoons chopped basil leaves

1 small red chile, seeded and finely chopped

150 g salted butter

makes 1¼ cups

Put the pine nuts in a small food processor, then grind as finely as possible. Add the remaining ingredients and pulse to mix. Transfer to a sheet of wax paper or plastic wrap and roll into a log. Alternatively, spoon into little butter dishes, smooth off the tops with a knife, then chill until firm.

EXTRA IDEAS

- Dill leaves and salted anchovy fillets
- Mint and fresh pomegranate juice
- Lovage and walnuts
- Fennel leaves and rose petals

- curry leaves or bay leaves (optional)
- cilantro
- mint

MINT AND CILANTRO SALSA WITH SINGARAS

1 lb. baking potatoes, cut into fries

8 curry leaves or 3 bay leaves

1 tablespoon vegetable oil,
plus extra for deep-frying

2 onions, finely chopped

2 garlic cloves, crushed

2 hottish green chiles,
seeded and finely chopped

1 teaspoon ground cumin

a small bunch of cilantro, chopped

16 small spring roll wrappers
(5 inches square), cut in 2
or 8 large (10 inches square), cut in 3

sea salt

salsa

5 pink Thai shallots or 2 regular,
finely chopped

finely grated zest and juice of 1 lime

½ teaspoon sugar (optional)

2 ripe mangoes, peeled and
cut into small cubes

2 red chiles, seeded and finely chopped

a handful of mint leaves, finely chopped

a handful of cilantro leaves, finely chopped

an electric deep-fryer (optional)

serves 6–8

Singaras are a kind of Indian samosa, but I make them with spring roll wrappers rather than heavier pastry dough. They are wonderful on their own, with a squeeze of lemon, or with a salsa like this one. Another idea is to put whole cilantro and mint leaves, and finely sliced red onion into small bowls, so people can take a little of each with a bite of singara—the result is a terrific snack to serve with drinks. Make them large or small.

Put the freshly cut potato fries in a saucepan of cold water, add the curry leaves, if using, bring to a boil, then add salt. When the potatoes are soft, drain and cover with a clean dish towel for 5 minutes, then remove the curry leaves and chop into the potatoes. Put in a bowl.

Heat the oil in a skillet, add the onions and garlic, and sauté until soft and very pale golden. Mash the potatoes, then stir in the onions, garlic, chiles, cumin, and chopped cilantro. Stir briefly and let cool.

Put a strip of spring roll wrapper on a work surface and put a teaspoon of mixture in the bottom left hand corner. Fold over to the right to make a triangle. Continue folding, end to end, then wet the edge with a little water and press to seal.

Fill a wok or deep-fryer one-third full with oil or to the manufacturer's recommended level and heat to 400°F. Add the singaras in batches of 2–3 and fry for about 2 minutes each, turning occasionally. Remove and drain on paper towels while you cook the remainder. They can be made in advance, and reheated in the oven, or served cold.

To make the salsa, put the shallots in a bowl, add the lime zest and juice, and sugar, if using, and set aside for 5 minutes. Just before serving, stir in the mango, chiles, mint, and cilantro. Serve with the singaras.

- basil
- thyme

TOMSATINA PICKLE
WITH THYME AND BASIL

24 ripe, well-flavored vine-ripened tomatoes, about 5 lb.

10 banana shallots, finely chopped

1 tablespoon allspice berries

3 tablespoons yellow mustard seeds

2 tablespoons thyme leaves

1¼ cups sugar

1¼ cups cider vinegar

a large bunch of basil, chopped

sea salt and freshly ground black pepper

4 preserving jars, 1 pint each, steriliized

makes about 2 lb.

This is one of my mother's favorite pickles. It's good to eat with strong organic farmhouse Cheddar-style cheese. In summer, just as the thyme is flowering, you should prune it hard, so it has another growth spurt before autumn. Then use the cuttings for recipes like these. Basil should be in full flavor at the same time.

Cut the tomatoes in half, cut out the cores, and chop the flesh. Put in a preserving pan and add the shallots and mustard seeds. Wrap the allspice in cheesecloth and add to the pan. Cook over gentle heat until the tomato juices start to run. Add the thyme, increase the heat, and simmer for about 45 minutes until reduced one-third.

Add the sugar and lower the heat until it dissolves. Add salt, pepper, vinegar, and basil. Increase the heat again and simmer until it thickens, about 30 minutes. Remove the cheesecloth-wrapped allspice berries. Use a bottling funnel to fill the sterilized jars while the pickle is still hot, but not boiling. Cover immediately with a circle of waxed paper and the lid. Tighten the lid when the pickle has cooled down a little.

Cook's extra This pickle is also good mixed with 1 tablespoon chopped black olives folded into 5 tablespoons of the pickle before serving. Serve with a young pecorino cheese and crisp Italian *carta de musica* as a snack with cocktails.

Note All pickles and preserves should be processed in a boiling water-bath canner according to USDA guidelines. For information, see website http://hgic.clemson.edu/factsheets/HGIC3040.htm

HERB VINEGARS

There are two methods for making herb-infused vinegars. Either push a sprig or two into the bottle and replace the lid, or boil 2 cups vinegar for every firmly packed cup of herb leaves. Pour over the leaves, set aside to infuse for 2 weeks, then strain and pour into sterilized bottles and seal with tight-fitting corks.

- White wine vinegar with **tarragon**

- Red wine vinegar with **rosemary**

- Cider vinegar with **apple mint**

- Rice vinegar with **Thai sweet basil**

- Champagne vinegar with rose petals or **rose geranium leaves**

- Push **lavender** flowers on long stems into white wine vinegar and leave on a window sill in full sun—the result is a delicious vinegar for salad dressing

HERB OILS

Any herb can be used to flavor oil, especially if you have large quantities of a particular herb in the garden and the hot sun has strengthened the volatile oils. I prefer to use the best-quality extra virgin olive oil, but any olive oil would do.

- The method for most woody herbs and tender leaves is simply to put a stem or two in the bottle and leave until the flavor is to your liking

- For soft herbs like basil, I also put the leaves in a blender (make sure they're not damp), add the oil, blend well, then leave to infuse overnight. Pour through a cheesecloth-lined strainer, pour into sterilized bottles, and use within 1 week. The color is wonderful

TISANES

A tisane is a herb tea, made with herbs, spices, or flowers infused in boiling water. For centuries, they have been used to treat illnesses, soothe the nerves, wake people up, or just because they taste good. Try these time-honored favorites.

- **Tulsi tisane** is made of **bush basil** or **holy basil**, called tulsi in India. It is a holy plant and was Krishna's favorite. He preferred the humble tulsi leaf to any of the flowers in the garden. In India, it isn't used for any other purposes other than those of a spiritual nature—so I include this recipe for holy herbal tea given to me by a friend from an ashram near the ancient Indian city of Rishikesh.

Put a handful of basil leaves and the zest of 1 unwaxed orange in a teapot, add 2½ cups boiling water and let infuse. Serve sweetened with 2 teaspoons honey (optional).

- **Hyssop tisane** is said to be good for colds in the chest.

Put a handful of hyssop leaves in a teapot, add 2½ cups boiling water and leave to infuse. Serve sweetened with 2 teaspoons of honey (optional).

Variations

- **Ginger tea** or **peppermint** tea to soothe an upset stomach

- **Lemon balm** (melissa) tea to invigorate

- **Rosemary**, especially when infused with honey, not only tastes good but helps with physical and mental strain (and is better for you than that caffeine-laden cappuccino)

- Another morning reviver is **lemon verbena** with **peppermint** and **rose petals**

OTHER THINGS TO DO WITH HERBS …

• Don't forget the flowers from your herbs such as **basil** or **marjoram**. Sprinkle them over dishes before serving—they are all edible, full of flavor, and very pretty

• Keep stalks of **parsley** and **chervil** to add to stocks, when boiling potatoes and vegetables, or to infuse in cream for sauces

• Stalks and roots of **cilantro** are full of flavor, so in many dishes, I chop most of the stalk and include it, too. When you buy cilantro in Asian and Middle Eastern markets, the roots will still be intact. Use them to make Thai curry paste, but freeze if you can't use them right away

• Use **rosemary** and **bay leaf** stalks as kabob skewers

• Branches of **fennel**, **rosemary**, **bay leaves**, **thyme**, **oregano** and **marjoram** are all delicious when thrown on the dying embers of a charcoal grill. Remember, you want smoke not flame to flavor the food, so add them just before the food is completely cooked otherwise the flames will blacken it. Alternatively, before cooking, push them into the cavity of a fish or chicken to flavor the flesh

• Make ice cubes with whole herb leaves and chive flowers (left) and add to water pitchers. **Borage** flowers are beautiful used this way

• Chop leaves and flowers and freeze in ice cube trays for stocks and soups

• Candy leaves such as **scented geraniums**, **mint**, **sweet cicely**, **basil**, **lemon balm**, and **pineapple sage**, and the petals and flowers of roses, **borage**, violas, and violets. Paint them with lightly whisked egg white and dust with sugar, arrange on a wire rack lined with parchment paper, and put in a warm dry place to harden. Store in an airtight container until ready to use

• Strew handfuls of **chervil**, **parsley**, **basil**, **mint**, and **cilantro** leaves on top of dishes, then fold in just before serving

• Wilt soft, young leaves of **oregano**, **chervil**, **parsley**, **tarragon**, **shiso**, or **basil** into hot pasta

• Roast peanuts or cashews and, while still burning hot, sprinkle with chiles and lots of **Chinese chives** and their flowers for a party snack to serve with cold beer

• Make thin sandwiches with fresh whole-wheat bread, thick butter and handfuls of soft herbs, such as **parsley**, **chervil**, **basil**, **tarragon**, and **watercress**. Cut into squares to eat with herbal tea or just as a little snack with some real lemonade on a picnic

• Use **thyme**, **fennel**, or **rosemary** to flavor jars of olives in oil

• Serve mixed bowls of **tarragon**, **mint**, **basil**, **parsley**, and **watercress**—in fact, any soft-leaf mixture—with wedges of feta and flat crispbread. An old Iranian tradition tells women to eat this at the end of a meal to keep their men from the attentions of rivals

• Make fresh *herbes de Provence* with **thyme**, **savory**, **oregano**, and **hyssop**

• Chop **lavender** flowers and roast with root vegetables

Bouquets garnis are traditional flavorings for casseroles:

• To make a bouquet garni for meat, make a bunch of 2 sprigs of **parsley**, 4 sprigs of **thyme**, 2 **bay leaves**, and 1 celery stalk, then tie together with twine. Discard before serving

• To make a bouquet garni for fish, make a bunch of 4 sprigs of **fennel**, 4 sprigs of **parsley**, and 4 sprigs of **marjoram**, then tie together with twine. Discard before serving

• To make a bouquet garni for chicken, make a bunch of 4 sprigs of **tarragon**, 2 **bay leaves**, a strip of fennel or celery, then tie together with twine. Discard before serving

Herb-flavored vodka is a 500-year-old tradition:

• Put 6 sprigs of **tarragon** into a bottle of vodka. Infuse for 36 hours at room temperature. Strain out and discard the leaves, then freeze the vodka for at least 5 hours before serving

• Put a handful of **wild ramps** with flowers into a bottle of vodka and proceed as above. For a touch of glamour, add a few fresh star-like flowers to the bottle before freezing

MAIL ORDER AND WEBSITES

ASSOCIATIONS

The Herb Society of America
9019 Kirtland Chardon Rd
Kirtland, Ohio 44094
(440) 256-0514
www.herbsociety.org

PLANTS & SEEDS

Avant Gardens
710 High Hill Road
Dartmouth, MA 02747
(508) 998-8819
www.avantgardensne.com
A complete selection of flowering perennial and herb plants.

The Banana Tree Inc.
715 Northampton St.
Easton, PA 18042
(610) 253-9589
www.banana-tree.com
A specialist in tropical plants and seeds with a diverse selection from around the world. They carry all the common herb seeds, plus uncommon seeds, such as capers.

Bluestone Perennials
7211 Middle Ridge Road
Madison, OH 44057-3096
(800) 852-5243
www.bluestoneperennials.com
Herb plants, sold in sets of three.

W. Atlee Burpee Seed Co.
300 Park Avenue
Warminster, PA 18974
(800) 888-1447
www.burpee.com
A wide selection of seeds from one of the country's oldest seed merchants. A good source for all the basics, but you can also find unusual seeds, such as pennyroyal and stevia.

Carroll Gardens
444 E. Main St.
Westminster, MD 21157
(800) 638-6334
www.carrollgardens.com

Companion Plants
7247 N. Coolville Ridge Rd.
Athens, OH 45701
(740) 592-4643
www.companionplants.com
A good selection of usual and unusual seeds and plants. For example, this company carries an unusual type of yarrow called garden mace (Achillea decolorans). This herb's foliage can be used like mace.

The Cook's Garden
PO Box 535
Londonderry, VT 05148
(800) 547-9703
www. cooksgarden.com
An excellent resource for the kitchen gardener. Plenty of seeds, and some plants. Much of their seed is certified organic.

Filaree Farm
182 Conconully Hwy
Okanogan, WA 98840
(509) 422 6940
www.filareefarm.com
Just garlic—more than 100 strains of organic seed garlic.

Goodwin Creek Gardens
PO Box 83
Williams, OR 97544
(800) 846-7359
www.goodwincreekgardens.com
Seeds and plants: culinary herbs, medicinal herbs, native American plants, plus an extensive selection of lavender.

Harris Seeds
355 Paul Rd
PO Box 24966
Rochester, NY 14624
(800) 514-4441

Heronswood Nursery
7530 NE 288th St.
Kingston, WA 98346
(360) 297-4172
www.heronswood.com
High-quality, eclectic selection of perennial plants.

Johnny's Selected Seeds
955 Benton Ave.
Winslow, ME 04910
(207) 861-3900
www.johnnyseeds.com
A full line of seeds for herbs, vegetables, and flowers, plus many growing and seed-starting accessories.

Nichols Garden Nursery
1190 Old Salem Rd. NE
Albany, OR 97321
(541) 928-9280
www.nicholsgardennursery.com
Known for its herb seeds, this company has introduced many distinctive new plants and seeds, including elephant garlic and "Betty's Blue" lavender. They offer a growing selection of certified organic seeds.

Park Seed
1 Parkton Ave.
Greenwood, SC 29647
(800) 213-0076
www.parkseed.com

Seeds of Change
PO Box 15700
Santa Fe, NM 87506
(888) 762-7333
www.seedsofchange.com
Extensive list of seeds for herbs, plus tools and accessories.

Select Seeds
180 Stickney Hill Rd.
Union, CT 06076
(860) 684-9310
www.selectseeds.com
Specializing in heirloom (open-pollinated) seeds.

Shepherd's Garden Seeds/White Flower Farm
30 Irene St.
Torrington, CT 06790
(860) 482-3638
www.shepherdseeds.com

Stokes
PO Box 548
Buffalo, NY 14240
(800) 396-9238
www.stokeseeds.com

Territorial Seed Company
PO Box 158
Cottage Grove, OR 97424
(541) 942-9547
www.territorialseed.com

The Thyme Garden
20546 Alsea Highway
Alsea, OR 97324
(541) 487-8671
www.thymegarden.com

NATURAL PEST CONTROL

Biocontrol Network
5116 Williamsburg Rd.
Brentwood, TN 37027
(800) 441-2847
www.biconet.com

Gardener's Supply Company
128 Intervale Rd.
Burlington, VT 05401
(888) 833-1412
www.gardeners.com
Earth-friendly solutions for common pest problems.

Gardens Alive
5100 Schenley Pl.
Lawrenceburg, IN 47025
(812) 537-8650
www.gardensalive.com
Innovative ideas for pest controls, including beneficial insects.

Peaceful Valley Farm Supply
P.O. Box 2209
Grass Valley, CA 95945
(888) 784-1722
www.groworganic.com

INDEX

CONVERSION CHARTS

Weights and measures have been rounded up
or down slightly to make measuring easier.

Volume equivalents:

American	Metric	Imperial
1 teaspoon	5 ml	
1 tablespoon	15 ml	
¼ cup	60 ml	2 fl.oz.
⅓ cup	75 ml	2½ fl.oz.
½ cup	125 ml	4 fl.oz.
⅔ cup	150 ml	5 fl.oz. (¼ pint)
¾ cup	175 ml	6 fl.oz.
1 cup	250 ml	8 fl.oz.

Weight equivalents: **Measurements:**

Imperial	Metric	Inches	Cm
1 oz.	25 g	¼ inch	5 mm
2 oz.	50 g	½ inch	1 cm
3 oz.	75 g	¾ inch	1.5 cm
4 oz.	125 g	1 inch	2.5 cm
5 oz.	150 g	2 inches	5 cm
6 oz.	175 g	3 inches	7 cm
7 oz.	200 g	4 inches	10 cm
8 oz. (½ lb.)	250 g	5 inches	12 cm
9 oz.	275 g	6 inches	15 cm
10 oz.	300 g	7 inches	18 cm
11 oz.	325 g	8 inches	20 cm
12 oz.	375 g	9 inches	23 cm
13 oz.	400 g	10 inches	25 cm
14 oz.	425 g	11 inches	28 cm
15 oz.	475 g	12 inches	30 cm
16 oz. (1 lb.)	500 g		
2 lb.	1 kg		

Oven temperatures:

110°C	(225°F)	Gas ¼
120°C	(250°F)	Gas ½
140°C	(275°F)	Gas 1
150°C	(300°F)	Gas 2
160°C	(325°F)	Gas 3
180°C	(350°F)	Gas 4
190°C	(375°F)	Gas 5
200°C	(400°F)	Gas 6
220°C	(425°F)	Gas 7
230°C	(450°F)	Gas 8
240°C	(475°F)	Gas 9